Leaving Certificate Higher Level Chemistry

The revised Leaving Certificate Chemistry syllabus was introduced in 2000 and was examined for the first time in 2002. Since that time, the examination paper has settled down into a standard format and has been marked in a consistent manner. The following key points should be studied carefully by you and will help you to perform to the best of your ability on the examination paper.

1. Requirements of the Examination Paper

Make sure that you are familiar with the requirements of the exam paper as well as the format (layout) of the paper. Of the 11 questions on the exam paper, **you must answer eight questions in three hours**, i.e. an average of 22.5 minutes per question. It is unwise to attempt more than eight questions as only your best eight questions will be taken into account so time spent on a ninth question is wasted. Make sure that you pick the eight questions in which you feel that you can perform best. In deciding your best 8 questions, it is very important to read each question thoroughly.

Section A consists of three questions based on the mandatory experiments. Section B consists of eight questions drawn from various other areas of the syllabus. It is also possible to be examined on the mandatory experiments in Section B. You must attempt at least two of the questions in Section A. When you have attempted two of the questions in Section A, you must attempt any six other questions from the remaining questions on the paper. You may attempt all three questions on practical work if you wish.

- **Questions 1–3** are based on the 28 mandatory experiments listed on the page opposite to page 1 of *Chemistry Live!*

- **Question 4** always consists of 11 short items and you must answer eight of these items. It is wise to attempt all of these short questions as your best eight questions will be taken into account.

- **Questions 5, 6, 7, 8** and **9** are full questions with no internal choice.

- **Questions 10** and **11** both consist of three parts of which you must attempt two parts.

These questions will be discussed in more detail at a later stage.

2. The Marking Scheme

The exam paper is marked by the examiner using a marking scheme. The entire paper is marked out of 400 marks. Since you must answer eight questions, this means that each question is worth 50 marks. Most marks are given in bundles of 3. Therefore, if you see that part of a question is worth 15 marks, this means that the examiner is usually looking for 5 points.

Since marks are allocated in bundles of 3, and each full question is worth 50 marks, this means that, in some cases, more than 3 marks are allocated to a point. For example, in question 4, each short question is worth 6 marks and an extra mark is added to the first two parts that you get fully correct. This increase in allocation of marks above 3 marks occurs in every question and is usually indicated on the paper. For example, the first part of questions 1, 2, 3, 5, 6, 7, 8 and 9 is usually assigned 5 or 8 marks. Also, in questions 10 and 11, you will see parts of questions allocated marks like 4, 5, 7 and 8.

3. Format of the Examination Paper

It is very important that you know the layout of the paper and the parts of the syllabus that will be examined in each question. When revising for the Leaving Certificate examination, it is wise to organise your revision around the exam itself, i.e. plan your revision on each section of the syllabus and the corresponding questions on past exam papers rather than revising chapter by chapter in the textbook.

D1725708

Section A

As already stated, questions 1, 2 and 3 in Section A are based on the 28 mandatory student experiments on the syllabus. The mandatory experiments that have been asked to date are shown in Table 1.

	Question 1	Question 2	Question 3
Sample paper (Feb 2002)	Concentration of sodium hypochlorite in bleach.	Extraction of clove oil.	Relative molecular mass of a volatile liquid.
2002	Concentration of ethanoic acid in vinegar.	Preparation of soap.	Effect of concentration on reaction rate.
2003	Concentration of iron in iron tablets.	Preparation of ethyne.	Determine the relative molecular mass of a volatile liquid.
2004	Determine hardness of water sample.	Preparation of ethene.	Recrystallisation of benzoic acid.
2005	Concentration of dissolved oxygen.	Preparation of ethanal.	Rate of decomposition of hydrogen peroxide.
2006	Determination of percentage of water of crystallisation in hydrated sodium carbonate.	Preparation of soap.	Determine concentration of chlorine in swimming-pool water.
2007	An iodine/thiosulfate titration.	Preparation and properties of ethanoic acid.	Determination of heat of reaction of HCl and NaOH.
2008	Determination of the concentration of ethanoic acid in vinegar	Chromatography, extraction of clove oil from cloves (or similar alternative) by steam distillation	Monitoring the rate of production of oxygen from hydrogen peroxide using manganese dioxide as a catalyst

Table 1 Mandatory experiments that have been examined in Section A.

Note that a clear pattern has been followed to date, i.e. Question 1 involves volumetric analysis, Question 2 tests your knowledge of the organic practical work and Question 3 is based on the other practicals outside the areas of volumetric analysis and organic practical work.

It is best to be prepared to answer all three questions on practical work in case your choice may be limited by the particular questions asked in Section B. Therefore, study your mandatory experiments very carefully!

Section B

Question 4

This question consists of 11 short questions and you must answer eight of these questions. It is advisable to attempt all 11 parts and your best eight will be taken into account by the examiner.

This question is a form of 'sweeper' question, i.e. it examines those areas that have not been examined in the full questions on other areas of the syllabus. Each question only involves a short answer so do not spend more than 2–3 minutes on each question. The questions typically involve stating definitions, giving short descriptions, stating brief contributions of scientists, drawing structural formulas, balancing equations, etc. This question is usually a very popular one and most students perform well on it.

Questions 5–9

The topics that have been examined on questions 5–9 (inclusive) are summarised in Table 2.

	Question 5	Question 6	Question 7	Question 8	Question 9
Sample paper (Feb 2002)	Periodic Table and Trends	Organic Chemistry	Thermochemistry	Instrumentation	Equilibrium
2002	Trends in Periodic Table	Organic Chemistry	Instrumentation	Fuels and Thermochemistry	Water and Sewage Treatment
2003	Atomic Structure, Chemical Bonding	Organic Chemistry	Rates of Reactions	Acids and Bases, Water Analysis	Organic Chemistry
2004	Chemical Bonding, Trends in Periodic Table	Fuels and Thermochemistry	Organic Chemistry	Rates of Reactions	Chemical Equilibrium
2005	Atomic Structure, Periodic Table, Chemical Bonding	Fuels and Thermochemistry	Organic Chemistry	Acids and Bases, Water and Sewage Treatment	Chemical Equilibrium
2006	Atomic Structure, Trends in Periodic Table	Fuels and Thermochemistry	Rates of Reactions	Hardness of Water, Acids–Bases Indicators	Organic Chemistry
2007	Atomic Structure, Chemical Bonding, Boiling Points.	Fuels	Acids and bases, pH calculations. Eutrophication and water treatment.	Organic Chemistry	Rates of Reactions.
2008	Trends in Periodic Table, Bonding	Fuels and Thermochemistry	Chemical Equilibrium	Self-Ionisation of Water, pH calculations, Water Treatment	Organic chemistry, Mechanisms of reactions

Table 2 Pattern of topics on questions 5–9 (inclusive).

Note from Table 2 that there are certain major topics that are examined consistently:

- Atomic Structure, Periodic Table, Chemical Bonding.
- Organic Chemistry
- Fuels and Thermochemistry
- Rates of Reactions/Chemical Equilibrium.
- Acids and Bases, pH, Water.

All of the above areas should be studied very carefully by you. Although the topic of Instrumentation is a minor topic on the syllabus, it has been given emphasis from time to time on the examination paper. So make sure you do not leave out this topic in your revision!

These are usually popular questions since they have an internal choice in each question, i.e. two out of three parts must be attempted. The topics that have been asked to date on questions 10 and 11 are summarised in Table 3.

	Question 10	**Question 11**
Sample paper (Feb 2002)	(a) Organic Chemistry (b) Rates of Reactions (c) Atomic Structure	(a) Water (b) Stoichiometry (c) Crystals or Industrial Chemistry
2002	(a) Oxidation and Reduction (b) Atomic Structure (c) Equilibrium	(a) Stoichiometry (b) Radioactivity (c) Industrial Chemistry or Extraction of Metals
2003	(a) Thermochemistry (b) Acids and Bases, pH (c) Flame tests and anion tests	(a) Equilibrium (b) Trends in the Periodic Table (c) Atmospheric Chemistry or Crystals
2004	(a) Stoichiometry (b) Atomic Structure (c) Properties of Gases	(a) Radioactivity (b) pH scale and calculations (c) Crystals or Atmospheric Chemistry
2005	(a) Stoichiometry (b) Trends in the Periodic Table (c) Instrumentation	(a) Oxidation–Reduction, Electrochemistry (b) Stoichiometry, Properties of Gases (c) Polymers or Atmospheric Chemistry
2006	(a) Instrumentation (b) Oxidation Numbers (c) Organic Chemistry	(a) Properties of Gases (b) Equilibrium (c) Industrial Chemistry or Extraction of Metals
2007	(a) Equilibrium (b) Stoichiometry (c) Oxidation and Reduction	(a) Atomic Structure, Radioactivity (b) Mechanisms of Reactions (c) Atmospheric Chemistry or Metals
2008	(a) Water Analysis and Tests for Anions (b) Oxidation and Reduction (c) Energy Levels and Atomic Structure	(a) Organic Chemistry (b) Stoichiometry (c) Atmospheric Chemistry or Metals

Table 3 Pattern of topics on questions 10 and 11.

Note from Table 3 that there are certain key areas that are regularly examined.
- Stoichiometry
- Industrial Chemistry/Atmospheric Chemistry **OR** Materials/Extraction of metals
- Properties of Gases.
- Acids and Bases, pH scale and calculations on pH

In addition, you may be examined in areas like Rates of Reaction, Equilibrium, Thermochemistry, Trends in the Periodic Table, Instrumentation, etc. depending on the extent to which these topics have been examined in the other main questions.

4. Terminology Used on the Examination Paper

The terms used on the examination paper and the marks allocated to each part of the question give you a good indication of the depth required when answering the question. The terms may be divided into a number of categories.

(i) Terms requiring a short answer

Words like *define, name, identify, state, what...? list, give*, etc. are commonly used to test your recall of material. Marking schemes indicate that a brief reply is required so simply state the answer and carry on to the next question. Some examples of this type of question are given in the box below:

Question:	Define electronegativity [2005 Q4(a)]
Answer:	Electronegativity is the relative attraction that an atom in a molecule has for the shared pair of electrons in a covalent bond.
Question:	What is the purpose of tertiary treatment? [2002 Q9(b)(ii)]
Answer:	The purpose of tertiary treatment of sewage is to remove phosphorus and nitrogen compounds.
Question:	List the following three types of radiation in order of increasing penetrating power: alpha- (α-), beta- (β-), gamma (γ-) [2003 Q4(f)]
Answer:	alpha, beta, gamma.
Question:	Identify two structural features of a hydrocarbon fuel which affect its octane number. [2004 Q6(e)]
Answer:	Octane number is affected by the **length** of chain, the degree of **branching** and whether the chain is a straight chain or a **cyclic** chain. (Any two of these three features was awarded full marks).
Question:	Give two ways in which you would expect the melting point of the impure benzoic acid to differ from that of the purified acid. [2004 Q3(b)(ii)]
Answer:	The impure benzoic acid melts at a lower temperature. The melting point of the impure benzoic acid is not sharp, i.e. it melts over a wider range of temperatures.
Question:	The conversion of B to A is an elimination reaction. What two features of elimination reactions are illustrated by this conversion? [2007 Q8(b)]
Answer:	The two features of elimination reactions are (i) a small molecule is removed from a larger molecule (in this case a molecule of water is removed from a molecule of ethanol) and (ii) a double bond is formed in the larger molecule.

(ii) Terms requiring a more detailed answer

Words like *discuss, explain, account for, describe* and *outline* are used to test your understanding of the topic. Since these terms require a more detailed answer, it is important that you give a number of points in your answer. Some examples of this type of question are given in the box below:

Question:	The oxidation of potassium sodium tartrate by hydrogen peroxide catalysed by cobalt(II) ions provides evidence for the intermediate formation theory of catalysis. State the observations you would make when carrying out this experiment. Explain how these observations provide evidence for the intermediate formation theory. (18) 2004 Q8(d)]
Answer:	The solution is pink at the beginning, then bubbling (effervescence) is observed, the pink colour changes to green and at the end of the reaction the green solution becomes pink again. The fact that the colour changes from pink to green indicates the formation of a new substance. As this new substance (green) changes back to its original colour (pink), this suggest that it is an intermediate.

> **Question:** In 1913 when Niels Bohr proposed his model for the structure of the atom, he made a number of assumptions. The most important was that electrons in atoms occupied fixed energy levels or shells and could only absorb or release energy by moving from one energy level to another. Outline the spectral evidence which exists to support this assumption for the hydrogen atom. (18) [Sample Paper 2002 Q10(c)]
>
> **Answer:**
> - The one electron in hydrogen is normally found in its lowest energy level (the ground state).
>   - When energy is supplied to an atom, a certain amount of the energy is absorbed and the electron moves into a higher energy level (an excited state).
>   - The electron soon falls back down to a lower energy level. When this occurs, a definite amount of energy (equal to the difference in energy between the two levels) is emitted.
>   - The energy of light is related to its frequency by the equation:
> $$E = h\,f. \qquad \text{(h = Planck's constant)}$$
>   - Each definite amount of energy emitted therefore corresponds to a specific frequency of light, which gives rise to a line of a particular colour in the emission spectrum.
>   - Since only definite amounts of energy are emitted, this implies that electrons can occupy only definite energy levels. Therefore, energy levels must exist in the atom.
>   - The values calculated by Bohr for the wavelengths of light emitted by hydrogen exactly match the values obtained by experiment.
>
> *Note: Since 18 marks are allocated to this question, at least six points are required. For a question that requires a lot of detail, it is better to give your answer in points than to attempt to write an essay-type description. Writing the answer in points makes it easier for the examiner to mark and helps you to ensure that you have covered all the main points.*

(iii) Terms requiring you to distinguish between items

If you are asked to distinguish between items, simply give a definition of each item.

> **Question:** Distinguish between the primary and secondary stages of sewage treatment. (12) [2002 Q9(b)(i)]
>
> **Answer:** Primary treatment is a mechanical process involving screening and settlement. Solids that are floating in the sewage are removed by passing the sewage through steel bars (screening). The sewage is stored in large tanks and solids settle to the bottom of the tank (settlement).
> Secondary treatment is a biological process in which the levels of suspended and dissolved organic materials are reduced. The sewage is pumped into a large aeration tank where micro-organisms digest the sewage (Activated Sludge Process) .
>
> **Question:** Distinguish between an atomic orbital and a sub-level. (6) [2005 Q4(e)]
>
> **Answer:** An atomic orbital is a region in space within which there is a high probability of finding an electron. A sub-level is a sub-division of a main energy level consisting of one or more orbitals of almost the same energy.
>
> **Question:** Distinguish between sigma (σ) and pi (π) covalent bonding. (6) [2007 Q4(d)]
>
> **Answer:** A sigma bond is a covalent bond formed by the head-on overlap of atomic orbitals.
> A pi bond is formed by the sideways overlap of atomic orbitals.

(iv) Miscellaneous items on marking schemes

From time to time some strange requirements appear on marking schemes. Some examples of these now follow:

(a) The question *Define first ionisation energy* [2002, Q5(a)] required the following in the marking scheme:

The first ionisation energy of an atom is the energy required to completely remove the most loosely bound electron (3) from a neutral gaseous atom (3) in its ground state (2).

For many years previously, full marks for this definition were always awarded for just the first two points. The final point ('in its ground state') had never been required before and is not found in any of the chemistry dictionaries! (In the former syllabus, each question was marked out of 66 marks. The problem with the above definition was that an extra 2 marks had to be found to make up the total marks to 50 marks in the new syllabus.)

(b) The marking scheme for the question on the decomposition of hydrogen peroxide on the 2001 Leaving Cert Higher Level Chemistry examination required the inclusion of a test tube containing manganese dioxide inside the flask as shown in Figure 1.

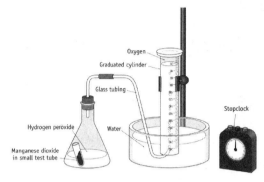

(c) In a question on the experiment to determine the amount of iron in an iron table [2003 Q1(a)], students were asked to explain *Why was it important to use dilute sulfuric acid as well as deionised water in making up the solution from the tablets?* (5)

Figure 1 Apparatus to monitor the rate of production of oxygen gas.

The acceptable answer was that the sulfuric acid helps to prevent the Fe^{2+} ions being oxidised to Fe^{3+} ions (3) by the oxygen in the air or oxygen dissolved in the water (2). (See *Chemistry Live!* page 193). Strangely, **hydrolysis** was not acceptable as an answer, despite the fact that it had been accepted in previous marking schemes.

(d) In a question which asked students to *Distinguish between a strong acid and a weak acid* [2007 Q7(a)], a strange requirement was made in the marking scheme for the definition of a weak acid.
Strong acid: A strong acid is a good proton donor, i.e. it is completely dissociated into ions in solution. (3)
Weak acid: A weak acid is a poor proton donor, i.e. it is slightly dissociated into ions in solution. (3)
Strangely, for the definition of a weak acid, students who used the phrase 'does not readily dissociate' obtained full marks but students who used the phrase 'does not fully dissociate' obtained no marks!

5. Revising for the Examination
The following points may be of help:
- Start revising in good time
- Make out a revision timetable and do your best to stick as closely as possible to it.
- As already stated, organise your revision around the structure of the examination paper.
- Do not leave out any section of the course. For example, if you find it difficult to solve problems on Equilibrium, you may be tempted to leave out this part of the course. However, you could be asked a question on Equilibrium in Question 4 or in Section A. At the very least, make sure you have studied the section on Equilibrium in *Rapid Revision Chemistry*.

6. The Examination Paper
When you get the examination paper, the advice that I give my own students is to start answering the questions on the mandatory experiments, i.e. answer the two questions in Section A that you feel most competent to tackle. When you have answered these two questions, carefully read through the rest of the paper and pick out the additional six questions that you are going to answer.

Take care with the terminology used on the paper. If you are asked to *name* a compound and you write down its formula, you are unlikely to be awarded any marks. Similarly, you will not get any marks if you are asked for the *formula* of a compound and you give the name instead! If you are asked to *identify* a compound, either the name or formula is acceptable.

It is absolutely vital that you show all your calculations clearly. Lay out your work so that the examiner can follow each step of your calculation. An example of how to lay out your work when solving a Thermochemistry problem is shown in the box on the following page.

Question: Given that the standard heats of formation of water, carbon dioxide and ethyne are −286, −394 and 277 kJ mol^{-1}, respectively, calculate the heat of combustion of ethyne. (12)
[Sample paper 2002 Q7(a)]

Answer:

<u>Required</u>: $C_2H_2 + 2\tfrac{1}{2}O_2 \rightarrow 2CO_2 + H_2O$

<u>Given</u>:

a	$H_2 + \tfrac{1}{2}O_2 \rightarrow H_2O$	$\Delta H = -286$ kJ/mol
b	$C + O_2 \rightarrow CO_2$	$\Delta H = -394$ kJ/mol
c	$2C + H_2 \rightarrow C_2H_2$	$\Delta H = +227$ kJ/mol

<u>Re-arrange</u>:

c reversed	$\Rightarrow$	$C_2H_2 \rightarrow 2C + H_2$	$\Delta H = -227$ kJ/mol
a	$\Rightarrow$	$H_2 + \tfrac{1}{2}O_2 \rightarrow H_2O$	$\Delta H = -286$ kJ/mol
b × 2	$\Rightarrow$	$2C + 2O_2 \rightarrow 2CO_2$	$\Delta H = -788$ kJ/mol
	$\Rightarrow$	$C_2H_2 + 2\tfrac{1}{2}O_2 \rightarrow 2CO_2 + H_2O$	$\Delta H = -1301$ kJ/mol

Answer: $\Delta H = -1301$ kJ/mol

- If you are asked a question like *State the colour change at the end point*, remember that you must write down TWO colours, i.e. the colour at the beginning and the colour when the end point has been reached. Do not get confused about the terms *clear* and *colourless*. Remember that a clear solution can be coloured, e.g. a solution of copper sulphate is blue.

- Pay particular attention to Organic Chemistry in your revision. It has a very important part on the exam paper.

- When asked to describe a procedure for a particular experiment, always number each step and leave a blank line between each step. Numbering each step will help you to mentally work through the procedure. Leaving the blank line helps you to fill in any point you may have forgotten.

- Always draw a labelled diagram when describing an experiment. A labelled diagram saves a lot of writing and is a very good way of earning marks. The labelled diagrams need only be in black and white as shown in the diagrams below.

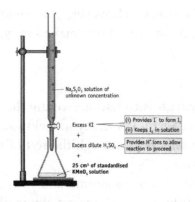

Figure 2(a) An iodine/thiosulphate titration.

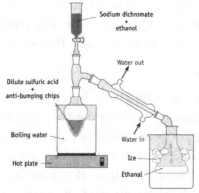

Figure 2(b) The laboratory preparation of ethanal.

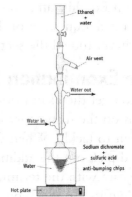

Figure 2(c) The preparation of ethanoic acid involves the use of reflux apparatus.

- If you are asked a question containing the phrase *What do you observe?* remember that you must describe what you **see** happening, e.g. bubbling, colour change, etc.

- Make sure you have learned the definitions required by the syllabus (boxed in *Chemistry Live!* and *Rapid Revision Chemistry*).

- When drawing a graph, make sure that you fill most of the page, that the axes are labelled with the name and units, and that the points on the graph are clearly shown. Also, if asked to calculate the instantaneous rate from the graph, do not forget to give the units of instantaneous rate!

- If asked for safety precautions for an experiment, use your common sense! For example, if you are preparing a flammable gas, then the gas preparation apparatus should be kept away from the Bunsen burner. Always wear safety glasses since, if there is a risk of an explosion, your eyes could be injured. Always use Quickfit apparatus or airtight stoppers to prevent gas escaping. Use heat resistant gloves to prevent burns when handling hot glassware.

- The question on volumetric analysis is usually very straightforward. An example of how to lay out your work is shown below.

Sample Paper 2002 Q1.

(a) Question: Explain why it was necessary to dilute the sample of bleach. (5)

Answer: Household bleach is too concentrated to be titrated directly. If the bleach were not diluted, excessive amounts of potassium iodide and sodium thiosulfate would be needed in the experiment.

(b) Question: Briefly describe the procedure for accurately diluting the sample of bleach to 250 cm^3. (12)

Answer:
1. Using a pipette filler, pipette 25 cm^3 of the concentrated bleach into a clean 250 cm^3 volumetric flask.

2. Add deionised water to the volumetric flask.

3. Bring the bottom of the meniscus up to the engraved mark on the neck of the volumetric flask.

4. When making the solution up to the mark, the water should be added drop by drop using either a wash bottle or a dropper or a pipette.

(c) Question: The student added approximately 20 cm^3 of dilute sulfuric acid and 10 cm^3 of 0.5 M potassium iodide to the conical flask containing the diluted bleach. What piece of apparatus is suitable to measure out these volumes of liquids? (3)

Answer: A graduated cylinder.

(d) Question: Why was an excess of potassium iodide necessary? What colour change was observed in the conical flask when the sulfuric acid and potassium iodide were added to the bleach? (6)

Answer: The I$^-$ ions must be kept in excess to ensure that the amount of iodine formed depends on the amount of hypochlorite present. An alternative answer is that I$^-$ ions are necessary in order to keep the I$_2$ formed in solution.
Colourless to reddish/brown colour.

(e) Question: Name the indicator used in this titration and describe how the end point was detected. When was the indicator added during the titration? (12)

Answer: Starch.

The end point is detected when the blue/black colour changes to colourless.
The indicator is added when the iodine solution in the conical flask is a pale yellow (straw) colour.

(f) Question: Calculate the concentration of sodium hypochlorite in the household bleach in moles per litre. Express this concentration in terms of %w/v. (12)

Answer: GIVEN

$$\boxed{ClO^-} \qquad \boxed{S_2O_3^{2-}}$$

$V_o = 25$

$M_o = ?$

$n_o = 1$

$V_r = 20.7$

$M_r = 0.21$

$n_r = 2$

$$\frac{25 \times M_o}{1} = \frac{20.7 \times 0.21}{2}$$

$$M_o = \frac{20.7 \times 0.21}{2 \times 25}$$

$$M_O = 0.087 \text{ moles per litre.}$$

∴ Concentration of original solution is 0.087×10

= 0.87 M

= 0.87×74.5 g NaClO per litre

= 64.82 g NaClO per litre

= 6.48 g NaClO per 100 cm^3

= 6.48 % w/v

Answer: Concentration of sodium hypochlorite in bleach = 0.87 M

= 6.48% w/v

By studying *Chemistry Live!*, working through the past exam papers in this book, studying the marking schemes on the State Examinations Commission website and using *Rapid Revision Chemistry*, you will be well prepared for the examination.

Bhail ó Dhia ar an obair! I wish you all the very best of luck!

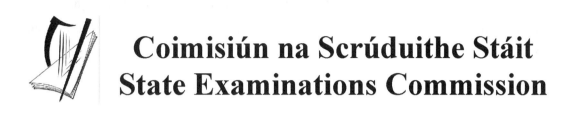

Coimisiún na Scrúduithe Stáit
State Examinations Commission

LEAVING CERTIFICATE EXAMINATION, 2008

CHEMISTRY – HIGHER LEVEL

THURSDAY, 5 JUNE – AFTERNOON 2.00 to 5.00

400 MARKS

Answer **eight** questions in all

These **must** include at least **two** questions from **Section A**

All questions carry equal marks (50)

Information

Relative atomic masses: H = 1, C = 12, O = 16

Universal gas constant, R = 8.3 J K^{-1} mol^{-1}

Molar volume at room temperature and pressure = 24.0 litres

Avogadro constant = 6×10^{23} mol^{-1}

Section A

Answer at least <u>two</u> questions from this section [see page 1 for full instructions].

1. To determine the concentration of ethanoic acid, **CH₃COOH**, in a sample of vinegar, the vinegar was first diluted and then titrated against 25.0 cm³ portions of a previously standardised 0.10 M solution of sodium hydroxide, **NaOH**. One rough and two accurate titrations were carried out.

   The three titration figures recorded were 22.9, 22.6 and 22.7 cm³, respectively.

   (*a*) Why was the vinegar diluted? (5)

   (*b*) Describe the correct procedures for measuring exactly 25.0 cm³ of vinegar and diluting it to exactly 250 cm³ using deionised water. (15)

   (*c*) The equation for the titration reaction is:

$$CH_3COOH \ + \ NaOH \ \longrightarrow \ CH_3COONa \ + \ H_2O$$

   Name an indicator suitable for this titration. Justify your choice of indicator.
   State the colour change at the end point. (12)

   (*d*) Calculate the concentration of the diluted solution of ethanoic acid in

   (*i*) moles per litre, (*ii*) grams per litre.

   State the concentration of ethanoic acid in the original vinegar sample in grams per litre.

   Express this concentration in terms of % (w/v). (15)

   (*e*) Ethanoic acid is a carboxylic acid. Identify the carboxylic acid which occurs in nettles and stinging ants. (3)

_____

2. Chromatography is widely used in chemistry as a separation technique.

(a) Describe, with the aid of clearly labelled diagrams, how you would set up and carry out an experiment to separate the components in a mixture of indicators using paper chromatography, thin-layer chromatography or column chromatography. (15)

(b) Explain why the different components of the mixture travel different distances along the paper or along the thin-layer or through the column in a given time. (6)

Steam distillation, using an apparatus like that shown, is a technique used to isolate an organic substance from plant material. The principle of this technique is that the boiling point of a mixture of two *immiscible liquids* is below the boiling points of both pure liquids. This allows the organic substance to be isolated at temperatures below 100 °C and avoids the delicate organic molecules being damaged at high temperatures.

(c) What is meant by the term *immiscible liquids*? (3)

(d) Name a substance you isolated by steam distillation in the school laboratory and the plant material from which it was extracted. (6)

(e) Explain the function of the tube labelled **X**. (6)

(f) Describe the appearance of the distillate collected. Name or describe briefly a technique that could be used to separate the organic substance from the water. (9)

(g) In a steam distillation experiment 20.0 g of plant material were heated in the presence of steam. Only 0.250 g of pure organic liquid was obtained. Calculate the percentage yield. (5)

———————————————

3. (a) Hydrogen peroxide solution is an oxidising reagent. Draw *or* describe the warning symbol put on a container of hydrogen peroxide solution to indicate this hazard. (5)

(b) Write a balanced equation for the decomposition of hydrogen peroxide. (6)

(c) Solid manganese(IV) oxide catalyst was added to a hydrogen peroxide solution at a time known exactly and the rate of production of gas was monitored as the hydrogen peroxide decomposed. Draw a labelled diagram of an apparatus that could be used to carry out this experiment. (12)

(d) The table shows the volumes of gas (at room temperature and pressure) produced at intervals over 12 minutes.

Time / minutes	0.0	1.0	2.0	3.0	5.0	7.0	9.0	11.0	12.0
Volume / cm^3	0.0	20.0	36.0	50.5	65.5	73.0	76.5	78.0	78.0

Plot a graph of the volume of gas produced *versus* time.
Explain why the graph is steepest at the beginning. (15)

(e) Use your graph to
(i) determine the instantaneous rate of gas production at 5 minutes,
(ii) calculate the total mass of gas produced in this experiment. (12)

———————————————

13

Section B

[See page 1 for instructions regarding the number of questions to be answered.]

4. Answer **eight** of the following items (*a*), (*b*), (*c*), etc. (50)

   (*a*) Write the electron configuration (*s, p, etc.*) of the aluminium ion (Al^{3+}).

   (*b*) What contribution did Henry Moseley, the scientist shown in the photograph, make to the systematic arrangement of the elements in the periodic table?

   (*c*) Give **two** properties of alpha particles.

   (*d*) Name the type of spectroscopy, based on absorptions within a particular range of electromagnetic frequencies, and used as a 'fingerprinting' technique to identify organic and inorganic compounds.

   (*e*) Write the formula of (*i*) a substance which causes temporary hardness in water, (*ii*) a substance which causes permanent hardness in water.

   (*f*) Name **two** metals which act as catalysts in the catalytic converters of modern cars.

   (*g*) Account for the difference in bond angle between water (104.5 °) and methane (109.5 °).

   (*h*) Copy the diagram of an exothermic reaction profile into your answer book and mark clearly (*i*) the activation energy, (*ii*) ΔH for the reaction.

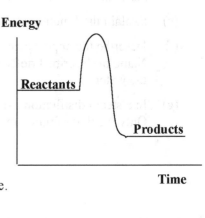

   (*i*) What is the purpose of tertiary treatment of sewage?

   (*j*) Complete and balance the equation:

$$C_2H_5OH \quad + \quad Na \quad \longrightarrow$$

   (*k*) Answer part **A** <u>or</u> part **B**.

     A   State the **two** main ways by which nitrogen is fixed in nature.

or

     B   State **two** ways in which steel differs from the iron produced in a blast furnace.

5. (*a*) Define *electronegativity*. (5)

   (*b*) State and explain the trend in electronegativity values down the first group in the periodic table of the elements. (9)

   (*c*) Use electronegativity values to predict the types of bonding (*i*) in water, (*ii*) in methane, (*iii*) in magnesium chloride. (9)

   (*d*) Use dot and cross diagrams to show the formation of bonds in magnesium chloride. (6)

   (*e*) Explain the term *intermolecular forces*. (6)

   (*f*) Use your knowledge of intermolecular forces to explain why methane has a very low boiling point (b.p. = −164 °C).
The relative molecular mass of methane is only slightly lower than that of water but the boiling point of water is much higher (b.p. = 100 °C). Suggest a reason for this. (6)

   (*g*) The diagram shows a thin stream of liquid flowing from a burette. A stream of water is deflected towards a positively charged rod whereas a stream of cyclohexane is undeflected. Account for these observations
Explain what would happen in the case of the stream of water if the positively charged rod were replaced by a negatively charged rod. (9)

---

6. (a) The hydrocarbon molecules in petrol typically contain carbon chains with between five and ten carbon atoms. The most widely used petrol in Ireland has an octane number of 95.

   (i) What is meant by the *octane number* of a fuel? (5)

   (ii) The two hydrocarbons used as references when establishing the octane number of a fuel are heptane and 2,2,4-trimethylpentane. Draw the structure of each of these molecules. (6)

   (iii) Crude oil is separated into a number of fractions in oil refining. Name the **two** fractions which contain molecules with the carbon chain lengths needed for petrol. (6)

   (iv) Dehydrocyclisation is one of the processes used to increase the octane numbers of hydrocarbons. What **two** changes to the hydrocarbon molecules occur during this process? (6)

   (v) Ethanol is an example of an oxygenate. Give another example of an oxygenate. Give **two** reasons why oxygenates are added to petrol. (9)

   (b) Write a balanced chemical equation for the combustion of ethanol, **C_2H_5OH**. Given that the heats of formation of ethanol, carbon dioxide and water are -278, -394 and -286 kJ mol^{-1}, respectively, calculate the heat of combustion of ethanol. (18)

   _____

7. A chemical equilibrium is established when eleven moles of hydrogen and eleven moles of iodine are mixed at a temperature of 764 K. Initially the colour of the mixture is deep purple due to the high concentration of iodine vapour. The purple colour fades and when equilibrium is established the colour of the mixture is pale pink and there are seventeen moles of hydrogen iodide present.

   The equilibrium is represented by the equation

   $$H_{2\,(g)} + I_{2\,(g)} \rightleftharpoons 2HI_{(g)} \qquad \Delta H = 51.8 \text{ kJ}$$
   $$\text{colourless} \qquad \text{purple} \qquad\qquad \text{colourless}$$

   (a) What is meant by *chemical equilibrium*?
   When the colour of the mixture has become pale pink, has reaction ceased? Explain. (11)

   (b) Write an expression for the equilibrium constant (K_c) for the reaction. (6)
   Calculate the value of the equilibrium constant (K_c) at 764 K. (12)

   (c) State *Le Châtelier's principle*. (6)

   Use Le Châtelier's principle to predict and explain the effect of a decrease in temperature on

   (i) the yield of hydrogen iodide, (ii) the intensity of colour of the equilibrium mixture. (9)

   What change, if any, will an increase in the pressure on the equilibrium mixture have on the yield of hydrogen iodide? Explain. (6)

   _____

8. (a) (i) Write an expression for the self-ionisation of water. (5)

   (ii) Define K_w, the ionic product of water.
   The value of K_w at 25 °C is 1.0×10^{-14}. Show that the pH of pure water is 7.0 at 25 °C. (12)

   (iii) Calculate the pH of a 0.5 M solution of a strong monobasic (monoprotic) acid.
   Calculate the pH of a 0.5 M solution of a weak monobasic acid with a K_a value of 1.8×10^{-5}. (12)

   (b) (i) Explain clearly how suspended solids are removed in the treatment of water for drinking. (9)

   (ii) Identify **two** chemicals added at the final stages of the treatment of water for drinking. State the purpose of adding each chemical you have identified. (12)

   _____

15

9. The alkenes are a homologous series of *unsaturated* hydrocarbons. Ethene (C_2H_4) is the first member of the series. Alkenes undergo addition reactions and polymerisation reactions.

(*a*)   Draw a labelled diagram of an apparatus used to prepare ethene gas in the school laboratory.   (8)

(*b*)   Draw the structure of any one of the isomers of the third member of the alkene series. Indicate clearly which carbon atoms have planar bonding and which are bonded tetrahedrally.   (12)

(*c*)   Explain the term *unsaturated*.   (6)

(*d*)   The ionic addition mechanism for the reaction of ethene with bromine water involves the formation of an intermediate ionic species. Draw the structure of this species.

Give the names or structural formulas of the three products that would be formed if the bromine water used in the reaction contained sodium chloride.

How does the formation of these three products support the mechanism of ionic addition?   (18)

(*e*)   Name the polymer formed when ethene undergoes addition polymerisation.
Draw **two** repeating units of this polymer.   (6)

_____

10.   Answer any **two** of the parts (*a*), (*b*) and (*c*).   (2 × 25)

(*a*)   A student is given a bucket of seawater.

(*i*)   Describe how the student could determine by filtration the total suspended solids (expressed as ppm) in the water.   (9)

(*ii*) How could the student determine the total dissolved solids (expressed as ppm) in a sample of the filtered seawater?   (9)

(*iii*) Describe a test to confirm the presence of the chloride ion in aqueous solution.   (7)

(*b*)   Define oxidation in terms of (*i*) electron transfer, (*ii*) change in oxidation number.   (7)

(*iii*) For the redox reactions shown below, use oxidation numbers to identify the species oxidised in the first reaction and the oxidising reagent in the second reaction.   (6)

$$ClO^- + I^- + H^+ \longrightarrow Cl^- + I_2 + H_2O$$

$$I_2 + S_2O_3^{2-} \longrightarrow I^- + S_4O_6^{2-}$$

(*iv*) Using oxidation numbers or otherwise balance both equations.   (12)

(*c*)   (*i*)   Define *energy level*.   (4)

(*ii*) Distinguish between *ground state* and *excited state* for the electron in a hydrogen atom.   (6)

The diagram shows how Bohr related the lines in the hydrogen emission spectrum to the existence of atomic energy levels.

(*iii*) Name the series of lines in the visible part of the line emission spectrum of hydrogen.   (3)

(*iv*) Explain how the expression $E_2 - E_1 = hf$ links the occurrence of the visible lines in the hydrogen spectrum to energy levels in a hydrogen atom.   (12)

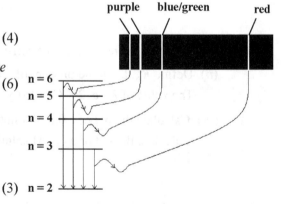

16

11. Answer any **two** of the parts (*a*), (*b*) and (*c*). (2 × 25)

(*a*) Alcohols can be obtained by the reduction of aldehydes and ketones using hydrogen and a suitable catalyst.

(*i*) Name a suitable catalyst for these reduction reactions. (4)

(*ii*) Name the alcohol produced when propanal (C_2H_5CHO) is reduced. (3)

(*iii*) Draw the structure of the alcohol produced when propanone (CH_3COCH_3) is reduced. To which class (primary, secondary or tertiary) of alcohols does it belong? (6)

(*iv*) Which of the two compounds, propanal or propanone, would be oxidised by warm Fehling's solution? Give the name *and* structure of the organic product of the oxidation reaction. (9)

(*v*) Give **one** common use for propanone. (3)

(*b*) From July 2008 changes will apply to the way in which taxes are levied on new cars bought in Ireland. Vehicles that, in controlled tests, have higher levels of carbon dioxide emission per kilometre travelled will be subject to higher levels of taxation. The measures are designed to encourage the purchase of cars that are more fuel-efficient and have lower CO_2 emissions.

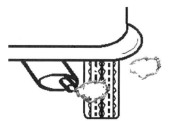

The manufacturer's specification for a certain diesel-engined car is 143 g CO_2 / km (i.e. the car produces 143 g of CO_2 for every kilometre travelled). The car is used for morning and afternoon school runs totalling 8 km per day.

Use the manufacturer's CO_2 emission figure to calculate the amount of CO_2 produced each day during the school runs in terms of

(*i*) the mass of CO_2, (*ii*) the number of moles of CO_2,

(*iii*) the volume of CO_2 at room temperature and pressure. (18)

If a large SUV (sports utility vehicle) with a CO_2 emission rating of 264 g CO_2 / km were used instead of the car mentioned above, how many more litres of CO_2 would be released into the atmosphere per day during the school runs? (7)

(*c*) Answer part **A** *or* part **B**

A

In 2007 former US Vice-President Al Gore and the UN Climate Change Committee were awarded the Nobel Peace Prize for their work in highlighting climate change. Al Gore has stressed the need to control global carbon dioxide emissions. Carbon dioxide is a *greenhouse gas* and an *acidic oxide*.

(*i*) Explain the underlined terms. (7)

(*ii*) State **two** major ways by which human activities contribute to the addition of carbon dioxide to the atmosphere. (6)

Al Gore

(*iii*) Carbon dioxide is removed from the atmosphere when it dissolves in rainwater, in seas, in lakes, etc.
What <u>three</u> chemical species form as a result of carbon dioxide gas dissolving in water? (9)

(*iv*) Acidic oxides can be removed from waste gases by scrubbers in chimneys before the gases are released into the atmosphere. Name a reagent used in scrubbers to remove acidic oxides. (3)

or

B

(*i*) Name the ore from which aluminium is extracted. What substance is used to convert this ore into a soluble aluminium compound in the first stage of the extraction? (7)

(*ii*) Write balanced equations for the reactions taking place at the positive and negative electrodes in the electrolysis of alumina. (12)

(*iii*) What is the function of cryolite (Na_3AlF_6) in the electrolysis of alumina? (3)

(*iv*) Why is recycling of aluminium metal important for the protection of the environment? (3)

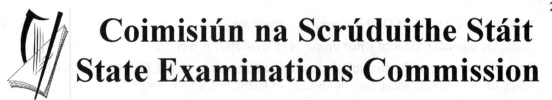

Coimisiún na Scrúduithe Stáit
State Examinations Commission

LEAVING CERTIFICATE EXAMINATION, 2007

CHEMISTRY - HIGHER LEVEL

TUESDAY, 19 JUNE – AFTERNOON 2.00 TO 5.00

400 MARKS

Answer **eight** questions in all

These **must** include at least **two** questions from **Section A**

All questions carry equal marks (50)

Information

Relative atomic masses: H = 1, He = 4, C = 12, O = 16, Na = 23, S = 32, Cr = 52, Fe = 56

Avogadro constant = 6×10^{23} mol^{-1}

Universal gas constant, $R = 8.3$ J K^{-1} mol^{-1}

Section A

Answer at least <u>two</u> questions from this section [see page 1 for full instructions].

1. A solution of sodium thiosulfate was prepared by weighing out a certain mass of crystalline sodium thiosulfate ($Na_2S_2O_3.5H_2O$) on a clock glass, dissolving it in deionised water and making the solution up carefully to 500 cm^3 in a volumetric flask. A burette was filled with this solution and it was then titrated against 25.0 cm^3 portions of previously standardised 0.05 M iodine solution in a conical flask. The average titre was 20.0 cm^3.

    The equation for the titration reaction is

    $$2S_2O_3^{2-} \quad + \quad I_2 \quad \rightarrow \quad 2I^- \quad + \quad S_4O_6^{2-}$$

    (a) Sodium thiosulfate is not a <u>primary standard</u>. Explain fully the underlined term. (8)

    (b) Describe how the crystalline thiosulfate was dissolved, and how the solution was transferred to the volumetric flask and made up to exactly 500 cm^3. (15)

    (c) Pure iodine is almost completely insoluble in water. What must be added to bring iodine into aqueous solution? (3)

    (d) A few drops of freshly prepared starch solution were added near the end point as the indicator for this titration. What sequence of colours was observed in the conical flask from the start of the titration until the end point was reached? (12)

    (e) Calculate the molarity of the sodium thiosulfate solution and its concentration in grams of crystalline sodium thiosulfate ($Na_2S_2O_3.5H_2O$) per litre. (12)

---

2. A sample of ethanoic acid (CH_3COOH) was prepared by the oxidation of ethanol using the apparatus shown. The reaction is exothermic and is represented by the following equation:

    $$3C_2H_5OH + 2Cr_2O_7^{2-} + 16H^+ \rightarrow 3CH_3COOH + 4Cr^{3+} + 11H_2O$$

    (a) Before heating the reaction flask, the ethanol and water were added from the tap funnel.
    State **two** precautions which should be taken when carrying out this addition in order to avoid excessive heat production. (8)

    (b) Describe and explain the colour change observed in the reaction flask as the ethanol was oxidised. (9)

    (c) What was the purpose of heating the reaction mixture under reflux after the addition from the tap funnel was complete? (6)

    (d) Show clearly that the ethanol was the limiting reagent when 8.0 cm^3 of ethanol (density 0.80 g cm^{-3}) was added to 29.8 g of sodium dichromate, $Na_2Cr_2O_7.2H_2O$. There was excess sulfuric acid present. (12)

    (e) Describe how the ethanoic acid product was isolated from the reaction mixture. (6)

    (f) Describe your observations when a small quantity of solid sodium carbonate was added to a sample of the ethanoic acid produced. Write a balanced chemical equation for the reaction which occurred. (9)

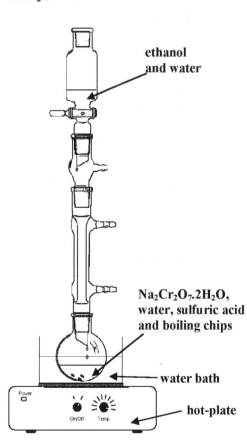

ethanol and water

$Na_2Cr_2O_7.2H_2O$, water, sulfuric acid and boiling chips

water bath

hot-plate

3. In an experiment to measure the heat of reaction for the reaction between sodium hydroxide with hydrochloric acid, a student added 50 cm³ of 1.0 M **HCl** solution to the same volume of 1.0 M **NaOH** solution in a polystyrene foam cup.

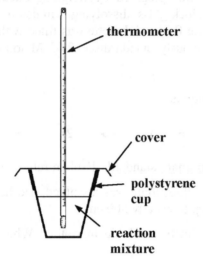

(a) To achieve an appreciable temperature rise during the reaction, quite concentrated solutions of acid and base, carrying the label illustrated, were used. What word describes the chemical hazard illustrated in this label? State **one** precaution the student should take when using these solutions. (8)

(b) The student had a choice of using either a graduated cylinder or a burette to measure out the solutions used in this experiment. Which piece of apparatus should have been used to achieve the more accurate result? (3)

(c) If the hydrochloric acid and sodium hydroxide solutions had been stored at slightly different temperatures, explain how the initial temperature of the reaction mixture could have been obtained. (6)

(d) List **three** precautions which should have been taken in order to obtain an accurate value for the highest temperature reached by the reaction mixture. (9)

(e) What was the advantage of mixing the solutions in a polystyrene foam cup rather than in a glass beaker or in a metal calorimeter? (3)

(f) Calculate the number of moles of acid neutralised in this experiment.
Taking the total heat capacity of the reaction mixture used in this experiment as 420 J K⁻¹, calculate the heat released in the experiment if a temperature rise of 6.7 °C was recorded.
Hence calculate the heat of reaction for

$$NaOH + HCl \rightarrow NaCl + H_2O$$ (18)

(g) Name the piece of apparatus used in industry to accurately measure the heats of combustion of foods and fuels. (3)

Section B

[See page 1 for instructions regarding the number of questions to be answered].

4. Answer **eight** of the following items (*a*), (*b*), (*c*), etc.   (50)

    (*a*) Define *atomic (covalent) radius*.

    (*b*) What is the principal use made of oxygenates such as methyl *tert*-butyl ether, MTBE, in the petrochemicals industry?

    (*c*) Distinguish between sigma (σ) and pi (π) covalent bonding.

    (*d*) What is meant by *heterogeneous* catalysis?

    (*e*) How many iron atoms should be consumed daily to meet the recommended daily intake of iron in the diet of 0.014 g?

    (*f*) Name the two reagents used in the brown ring test for the nitrate ion.

    (*g*) Name and draw the structure of a carboxylic acid that is widely used as a food preservative.

    (*h*) A 500 cm^3 can of beer contains 21.5 cm^3 of ethanol. Calculate its % alcohol, i.e. the concentration of alcohol in the beer as a % (v/v).

    (*i*) Explain in terms of bonding why it is more correct to represent the benzene molecule as

    instead of or

    (*j*) Ultraviolet absorption spectroscopy can be used in the quantitative analysis of some organic compounds (e.g. drug metabolites and plant pigments). What is the underlying principle of this analytical technique?

    (*k*) Answer part **A** <u>or</u> **B**.

        A   The use of CFCs as refrigerant gases has been discontinued. Name a group of substances used to replace CFCs as refrigerant gases.

    or

        B   Name the electrochemist who was the first to isolate the elements sodium and potassium in 1807 by passing electricity through sodium hydroxide and potassium hydroxide, respectively.

    _____

5. (*a*) Define *energy level*.   (5)

    Write the electron configuration (*s*, *p*) for the sulfur atom in its ground state, showing the arrangement in atomic orbitals of the highest energy electrons.   (6)
    State how many (*i*) energy levels, (*ii*) orbitals, are occupied in a sulfur atom in its ground state.   (6)

    (*b*) Use electronegativity values (Mathematical Tables p 46) to predict the type of bond expected between hydrogen and sulfur.
    Write the chemical formula for hydrogen sulfide.
    Use clear dot and cross diagrams to show the bonding in hydrogen sulfide.   (15)

    Would you expect the hydrogen sulfide molecule to be *linear* or *non-linear* in shape?
    Justify your answer.   (6)

    (*c*) Hydrogen sulfide has a boiling point of 212.3 K and water has a boiling point of 373 K.
    Account for the difference in the boiling points of these substances.   (6)
    Would you expect hydrogen sulfide to be soluble in water? Explain your answer.   (6)

    _____

6. Useful hydrocarbons are obtained by the fractional distillation of crude oil, which itself has little or no direct use. Hydrocarbons are excellent fuels.

    (*a*) In which fraction of crude oil do pentane and its isomers occur? (5)

    Give the systematic (IUPAC) name of each of the structural isomers of pentane shown below. (9)

    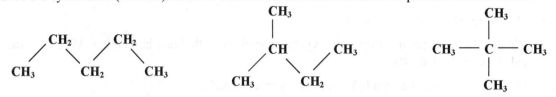

    Which of these isomers would you predict to have the lowest octane number?
    Justify your choice in terms of the structural features of the molecules. (9)

    Write a balanced equation for the combustion of pentane (C_5H_{12}) in excess oxygen. (6)

    (*b*) Naphtha and gas oil are two of the hydrocarbon fractions obtained from the fractional distillation of crude oil. How do the molecules of the naphtha fraction differ from the molecules of the gas oil fraction? (3)

    Explain with the aid of a labelled diagram how naphtha (b.p. approximately 100 °C) is separated from gas oil (b.p. approximately 300 °C) in the fractional distillation of crude oil. (9)

    Bitumen is a residue fraction obtained from crude oil. Give **one** use for bitumen. (3)

    (*c*) What is catalytic cracking? What is its economic importance in oil refining? (6)

    _____

7. (*a*) Define (*i*) *acid*, (*ii*) *conjugate pair*, according to the Brønsted-Lowry theory. (8)

    Identify the two conjugate pairs in the following dissociation of nitrous acid (HNO_2):

    $$HNO_2 \;+\; H_2O \;\rightleftharpoons\; NO_2^- \;+\; H_3O^+$$ (6)

    Distinguish between a strong acid and a weak acid. (6)

    (*b*) Calculate the pH of 0.1 M nitrous acid (HNO_2); the value of the acid dissociation constant (K_a) for nitrous acid is 5.0×10^{-4}.

    What is the pH of a nitric acid (HNO_3) solution of the same concentration? (15)

    (*c*) *Eutrophication* in water may result from the addition of large quantities of nitrate fertilizers to it.

    Describe the processes occurring in the water leading to eutrophication. (9)

    (*d*) Explain how heavy metal ions are removed from large quantities of water. (6)

    _____

8. Study the reaction scheme and answer the questions which follow.

    $$C_2H_4 \;\underset{\longleftarrow}{\overset{\longrightarrow}{}}\; C_2H_5OH \;\underset{\longleftarrow}{\overset{\longrightarrow}{}}\; CH_3CHO$$

    $$\;\;\;\;A\;\;\;\;\;\;\;\;\;\;\;\;\;\;\;\;\;\;B\;\;\;\;\;\;\;\;\;\;\;\;\;\;\;\;\;\;C$$

    (*a*) Name the homologous series (*i*) to which **A** belongs, (*ii*) to which **C** belongs. (8)

    (*b*) The conversion of **B** to **A** is an elimination reaction. What two features of elimination reactions are illustrated by this conversion? (6)

    (*c*) Name the reagent and the catalyst required to convert **C** to **B**. (6)

    (*d*) Draw full structural formulas for **B** and **C**. Indicate any carbon atom in either structure that has planar geometry. List the bonds broken in **B** and the bond made in **C** in the synthesis of **C** from **B**. (18)

    (*e*) After carrying out a laboratory conversion of **B** to **C**, how could you test the product to confirm the formation of **C**? (9)

    (*f*) Compound **C** is formed as a metabolite of compound **B** in the human body. How does compound **B** come to be present in the body? (3)

22

9. (*a*) Define the *rate of a chemical reaction*.
Why does the rate of chemical reactions generally decrease with time? (8)

(*b*) The rate of reaction between an excess of marble chips (**CaCO₃**) (diameter 11 – 15 mm) and 50 cm³ of 2.0 M hydrochloric acid was monitored by measuring the mass of carbon dioxide produced.

The table shows the total mass of carbon dioxide gas produced at stated intervals over 9 minutes.

Time/minutes	0.0	1.0	2.0	3.0	4.0	5.5	7.0	8.0	9.0
Mass of CO_2/g	0.00	0.66	1.20	1.60	1.90	2.10	2.18	2.20	2.20

Plot a graph of the mass of carbon dioxide produced *versus* time. (12)

Use the graph to determine
(*i*) the instantaneous rate of reaction in grams per minute at 4.0 minutes,
(*ii*) the instantaneous rate of reaction at this time in moles per minute. (9)

(*c*) Describe and explain the effect on the rate of reaction of repeating the experiment using 50 cm³ of 1.0 M hydrochloric acid and the same mass of the same size marble chips. (6)

(*d*) Particle size has a critical effect on the rate of a chemical reaction.

(*i*) Mark clearly on your graph the approximate curve you would expect to plot if the experiment were repeated using 50 cm³ of 2.0 M HCl and using the same mass of marble chips but this time with a diameter range of 1 – 5 mm. (6)

(*ii*) Dust explosions present a risk in industry. Give **three** conditions necessary for a dust explosion to occur. (9)

---

10. Answer any **two** of the parts (*a*), (*b*) and (*c*). (2 × 25)

(*a*) (*i*) Write the equilibrium constant (**K_c**) expression for the reaction (7)

$$N_{2(g)} \;+\; 3H_{2(g)} \;\rightleftharpoons\; 2NH_{3(g)}$$

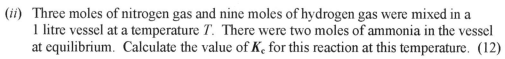

(*ii*) Three moles of nitrogen gas and nine moles of hydrogen gas were mixed in a 1 litre vessel at a temperature T. There were two moles of ammonia in the vessel at equilibrium. Calculate the value of K_c for this reaction at this temperature. (12)

(*iii*) Henri Le Chatelier, pictured on the right, studied equilibrium reactions in industry in the late 19th century. According to Le Chatelier's principle, what effect would an increase in pressure have on the yield of ammonia at equilibrium? Explain. (6)

(*b*) (*i*) State *Avogadro's law*. (7)

(*ii*) Carbon dioxide is stored under pressure in liquid form in a fire extinguisher. Two kilograms of carbon dioxide are released into the air as a gas on the discharge of the fire extinguisher. What volume does this gas occupy at a pressure of 1.01×10^5 Pa and a temperature of 290 K? (9)

What mass of helium gas would occupy the same volume at the same temperature and pressure? (6)

(*iii*) Give **one** reason why carbon dioxide is more easily liquefied than helium. (3)

(*c*) The halogens are good oxidising agents.

(*i*) How does the oxidation number of the oxidising agent change during a redox reaction? (4)

(*ii*) Assign oxidation numbers in each of the following equations to show clearly that the halogen is the oxidising agent in each case. (12)

$$Br_2 \;+\; 2Fe^{2+} \;\rightarrow\; 2Br^- \;+\; 2Fe^{3+}$$

$$Cl_2 \;+\; SO_3^{2-} \;+\; H_2O \;\rightarrow\; Cl^- \;+\; SO_4^{2-} \;+\; H^+$$

Hence or otherwise balance the second equation. (6)

(*iii*) Why does the oxidising ability of the halogens decrease down the group? (3)

11. Answer any **two** of the parts (*a*), (*b*) and (*c*). (2 × 25)

(*a*) In 1910 Rutherford (pictured right) and his co-workers carried out an experiment in which thin sheets of gold foil were bombarded with alpha particles. The observations made during the experiment led to the discovery of the atomic nucleus.

(*i*) Describe the model of atomic structure which existed immediately *prior* to this experiment. (7)

(*ii*) In this experiment it was observed that most of the alpha particles went straight through the gold foil. Two other observations were made. State these other observations and explain how each helped Rutherford deduce that the atom has a nucleus. (12)

In November 2006 former Soviet agent, Alexander Litvinenko, died in London. The cause of his death was identified as radiation poisoning by polonium-210.

(*iii*) Polonium-210 decays emitting an alpha particle.
Copy and complete the equation for the alpha-decay of polonium-210, filling in the values of *x* (atomic number), *y* (mass number) and **Z** (elemental symbol). (6)

$$^{210}_{84}\text{Po} \quad \rightarrow \quad ^{y}_{x}\text{Z} \quad + \quad ^{4}_{2}\text{He}$$

(*b*) An equimolar mixture of chlorine and methane react together at room temperature only when ultra-violet light is present.

(*i*) Explain clearly the role of the ultraviolet light in the reaction between chlorine and methane. (7)

(*ii*) Name the two main products of the reaction between chlorine and methane. (6)

(*iii*) Account for traces of ethane found in the product mixture. (6)

Chlorine reacts with ethene at room temperature even in the dark.

(*iv*) Name the type of mechanism which occurs in the reaction between chlorine and ethene. (3)

(*v*) Give a use for chloroalkanes. (3)

(*c*) Answer either part **A** *or* part **B**.

A

Environmentalists are concerned about the increasing abundance of carbon dioxide in the atmosphere.

(*i*) State one important way carbon dioxide is constantly added to the atmosphere. (4)

(*ii*) Carbon dioxide is a greenhouse gas. It has been assigned a <u>greenhouse factor</u> of 1.
What use is made of the *"greenhouse factor"* of a gas? (6)

(*iii*) Name **two** other greenhouse gases. (6)

(*iv*) Carbon dioxide is removed from the atmosphere when it dissolves in rainwater, seas, lakes, etc.
What **three** chemical species arise in water as a result of carbon dioxide gas dissolving in it? (9)

or

B

Aluminium, sodium chloride and graphite are all crystalline solids.

For each of these substances, name the type of crystal formed. (7)

Explain clearly, in terms of bonding, why

(*i*) aluminium is a good conductor of electricity,

(*ii*) sodium chloride is soluble in water,

(*iii*) graphite is soft and slippery. (18)

Coimisiún na Scrúduithe Stáit
State Examinations Commission

LEAVING CERTIFICATE EXAMINATION, 2006

CHEMISTRY - HIGHER LEVEL

TUESDAY, 20 JUNE - AFTERNOON 2.00 to 5.00

---

400 MARKS

Answer **eight** questions in all

These **must** include at least **two** questions from **Section A**

All questions carry equal marks (50)

Information

Relative atomic masses: H = 1, C = 12, O = 16, Na = 23, Ca = 40.

Universal gas constant, $R = 8.3$ J K^{-1} mol^{-1}

Molar volume at s.t.p. = 22.4 litres

Avogadro constant = 6×10^{23} mol^{-1}

Section A

Answer at least <u>two</u> questions from this section [see page 1 for full instructions].

1. An experiment was carried out to determine the percentage water of crystallisation and the degree of water of crystallisation, **x**, in a sample of hydrated sodium carbonate crystals ($Na_2CO_3.xH_2O$). An 8.20 g sample of the crystals was weighed accurately on a clock glass and then made up to 500 cm³ of solution in a volumetric flask. A pipette was used to transfer 25.0 cm³ portions of this solution to a conical flask. A previously standardised 0.11 M hydrochloric acid (**HCl**) solution was used to titrate each sample. A number of accurate titrations were carried out. The average volume of hydrochloric acid solution required in these titrations was 26.05 cm³.

The titration reaction is described by the equation:

$$Na_2CO_3 \quad + \quad 2HCl \quad \longrightarrow \quad 2NaCl \quad + \quad CO_2 \quad + \quad H_2O$$

(a) Identify a primary standard reagent which could have been used to standardise the hydrochloric acid solution. (5)

(b) Name a suitable indicator for the titration and state the colour change observed in the conical flask at the end point. Explain why not more than 1 – 2 drops of indicator should be used. (12)

(c) (i) Describe the correct procedure for rinsing the burette before filling it with the solution it is to deliver.

    (ii) Why is it important to fill the part below the tap of the burette? (12)

(d) From the titration figures, calculate the concentration of sodium carbonate (Na_2CO_3) in the solution in

    (i) moles per litre,

    (ii) grams per litre. (9)

(e) Calculate the percentage water of crystallisation present in the crystals and the value of **x**, the degree of hydration of the crystals. (12)

---

2. A sample of soap was prepared in the laboratory by refluxing a mixture of approximately 5 g of animal fat, 2 g of sodium hydroxide pellets (an excess) and 25 cm^3 of ethanol in an apparatus like that drawn on the right.

   (a) Why was the reaction mixture refluxed? Name the *type* of reaction which occurs during the reflux stage of the preparation. (8)

   (b) Complete and balance the equation below for the reaction between glyceryl tristearate, an animal fat, and sodium hydroxide. (9)

   $$C_{17}H_{35}COOCH_2$$
   $$|$$
   $$C_{17}H_{35}COOCH \quad\quad + \;\; 3NaOH \quad\quad \longrightarrow$$
   $$|$$
   $$C_{17}H_{35}COOCH_2$$

   glyceryl tristearate

   (c) What is the purpose of the ethanol? Why is it desirable to remove the ethanol after reflux? Describe with the aid of a labelled diagram how you would remove the ethanol after the reflux stage of the experiment. (12)

   (d) Describe how a pure sample of soap was obtained from the reaction mixture. (9)

   (e) At the end of the experiment, what is the location
            (i) of the second product of the reaction,
            (ii) of the excess sodium hydroxide? (6)

   (f) What would you observe, upon shaking, if a little of the soap prepared in this experiment is added to   (i) a test tube containing deionised water,
                        (ii) a test tube containing mineral water from a limestone region? (6)

   _____

3. A number of tests were carried out on a sample of swimming pool water to test its quality.

   (a) A colorimetric experiment was used to estimate the concentration of free chlorine in the sample. What is the general principle of all colorimetric experiments? (8)

   (b) Identify a suitable reagent to test for free chlorine in swimming pool water and state the colour which develops when this reagent reacts with free chlorine. (6)

   (c) Describe briefly how you would estimate the concentration of free chlorine in a sample using either a comparator <u>or</u> a colorimeter. (12)

   (d) Give the name <u>or</u> formula of a *free chlorine* species in the swimming pool water. Give a reason why the concentration of free chlorine in treated drinking water is usually between 0.2 - 0.5 p.p.m. whereas in swimming pool water it should be between 1 - 5 p.p.m. (9)

   (e) When 1200 cm^3 of swimming pool water was filtered, the mass of the filter paper, upon drying, had increased by 0.78 g. When 250 cm^3 of the filtered water was evaporated to dryness the mass of the residue obtained was 0.32 g. Calculate the concentration in p.p.m.
              (i) of suspended solids,
              (ii) of dissolved solids. (15)

   _____

Section B

[See page 1 for instructions regarding the number of questions to be answered.]

4. Answer **eight** of the following items (*a*), (*b*), (*c*), etc. (50)

   (*a*) Write the electron configuration (*s, p, etc.*) of a chromium atom in its ground state.

   (*b*) Name the scientist, shown in the photograph, who identified cathode rays as subatomic particles.

   (*c*) Give **two** differences between a nuclear reaction and a chemical reaction.

   (*d*) Calculate the percentage carbon, by mass, in methylbenzene.

   (*e*) What is (*i*) the conjugate acid and (*ii*) the conjugate base of H_2O?

   (*f*) What contribution did Newlands make to the systematic arrangement of the elements known to him?

   (*g*) What observation is made when a sample of ethanal is heated with Fehling's reagent?

   (*h*) The concentration of an aqueous solution of sodium hydroxide (**NaOH**) is 0.2 g per litre. Calculate its pH.

   (*i*) Under what circumstances can ionic compounds conduct electricity?

   (*j*) Which class of organic compound is responsible for the odour associated with fruits such as apples, oranges, pears, bananas and strawberries?

   (*k*) Answer part **A** or part **B**.

       A   State **two** uses of nitrogen gas based on its chemical stability.

   or

       B   Name **two** metals, one a main group metal, the other a transition element, both of which are protected from further corrosion by the oxide layer which forms on their surfaces.

---

5. (*a*) (*i*)   Describe how you would carry out a flame test on a sample of potassium chloride.   (8)

       (*ii*)   Why do different elements have unique atomic spectra?   (6)

       (*iii*) What instrumental technique is based on the fact that each element has unique atomic spectra?   (3)

   Bohr's model of the atom explained the existence of energy levels on the basis of atomic spectra. Bohr's theory was later modified to incorporate the idea of *orbitals* in recognition of the wave nature of the electron and Heisenberg's uncertainty principle.

       (*iv*) Define *atomic orbital*.   (6)

       (*v*)   What does Heisenberg's uncertainty principle say about an electron in an atom?   (6)

   (*b*) (*i*)   Define *electronegativity*.   (6)

       (*ii*)   Explain why there is a general increase in electronegativity values across the periods in the periodic table of the elements.   (6)

       (*iii*) Explain, in terms of the structures of the atoms, the trend in reactivity down Group I (the alkali metal group) of the periodic table.   (9)

---

6. (a) The table shows the octane numbers of four hydrocarbons.

Name	Formula	Octane No.
hexane	C_6H_{14}	25
cyclohexane	C_6H_{12}	83
benzene	C_6H_6	100
2,2,4-trimethylpentane	C_8H_{18}	100

   (i) What is meant by the octane number of a fuel? (8)

   (ii) Hexane has the lowest octane number of the four compounds listed. What structural feature of the molecule contributes to this? (3)

   (iii) In the case of each of the other three compounds, identify the structural feature of its molecules which contributes to it having a high octane number. (9)

   (iv) Name the process carried out in an oil refinery that converts hexane to compounds such as cyclohexane and benzene. Why is the use of benzene in petrol strictly controlled? (6)

   (b) (i) Give **two** reasons why oxygenates such as MTBE are added to petrol.
   (ii) Give **two** reasons why the addition of lead to petrol has been discontinued. (12)

   (c) The combustion of cyclohexane may be described by the following balanced equation:

   $$C_6H_{12(l)} + 9O_{2(g)} \longrightarrow 6CO_{2(g)} + 6H_2O_{(l)}$$

   Given that the heats of formation of cyclohexane, carbon dioxide and water are –156, –394 and –286 kJ mol^{-1}, respectively, calculate the heat of combustion of cyclohexane. (12)

---

7. (a) Define the *activation energy* of a chemical reaction. (5)

   (b) Give **two** reasons why the rate of a chemical reaction increases as the temperature rises. Which of these is the more significant? Why? (12)

   (c) Describe how you could investigate the effect of temperature on the rate of the reaction between a 0.1 M sodium thiosulfate solution and a 2 M hydrochloric acid solution. (12)
   The reaction is described by the following balanced equation.

   $$Na_2S_2O_3 + 2HCl \longrightarrow 2NaCl + SO_2 + S + H_2O$$

   (d) When silver nitrate and sodium chloride solutions are mixed a precipitate appears immediately. Explain the speed of this reaction compared to the slower reaction when solutions of sodium thiosulfate and hydrochloric acid are mixed. (6)

   (e) What type of catalysis occurs in the catalytic converter of a modern car?
   Give the names *or* formulas of **two** substances entering a car's catalytic converter <u>and</u> the names *or* formulas of the substances to which they are converted in the interior of the catalytic converter. (15)

---

8. (a) (i) What is *hard water*? (5)

   (ii) A supply of hard water is treated for domestic use by ion-exchange. You may assume that all the hardness is due to $Ca(HCO_3)_2$. Explain in words <u>or</u> using a balanced equation how a cation exchange resin, represented by **RNa**, softens this water supply. (6)

   (iii) In the treatment of water for drinking, what is meant by the term *flocculation*? Name a flocculating agent. (9)

   (iv) What substance is added to water to adjust the pH if the water is too acidic? Why is it undesirable to have the pH of drinking water below 6? (6)

   (b) (i) Explain how an acid-base indicator, which is itself a weak acid, and may be represented by **HX**, functions. (9)

   (ii) Draw a clearly labelled diagram of the titration curve you would expect to obtain when 50 cm^3 of a 0.1 M sodium hydroxide (**NaOH**) solution is added slowly to 25 cm^3 of a 0.1 M ethanoic acid (**CH$_3$COOH**) solution. (9)

   (iii) Explain with reference to your diagram why phenolphthalein is a suitable indicator for a titration of sodium hydroxide with ethanoic acid. (6)

9. The alkenes are a homologous series. Ethene (C_2H_4) is the first member of the series.

(a) What is meant by a *homologous series*? (5)

(b) Ethene may be made in a school laboratory using the arrangement of apparatus drawn on the right.

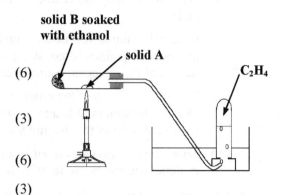

solid B soaked with ethanol

solid A

C_2H_4

   (i) Give the name <u>and</u> formula of the solid **A** which is heated using the Bunsen burner. (6)

   (ii) Identify the solid **B** which is used to keep the ethanol at the end of the test tube. (3)

   (iii) What precaution should be observed when heating is stopped? Why is this necessary? (6)

   (iv) Give **one** major use of ethene gas. (3)

(c) Describe the mechanism for the bromination of ethene. (9)
State and explain **one** piece of experimental evidence to support this mechanism. (6)

(d) Draw the structures <u>and</u> give the systematic (IUPAC) names for **two** alkene isomers of molecular formula C_4H_8. (12)

_____

10. Answer any **two** of the parts (a), (b) and (c) (2 × 25)

(a) (i) What are *isotopes*? (4)

   (ii) Define *relative atomic mass, A_r*. (6)

   (iii) What is the principle on which the mass spectrometer is based? (9)

   (iv) Calculate the relative atomic mass of a sample of lithium, given that a mass spectrometer shows that it consists of 7.4 % of ^{6}Li and 92.6 % of ^{7}Li. (6)

(b) Define *oxidation* in terms of change in oxidation number. (4)

What is the oxidation number of (i) chlorine in **NaClO** and (ii) nitrogen in NO_3^-? (6)

State and explain the oxidation number of oxygen in the compound OF_2. (6)

Using oxidation numbers or otherwise, identify the reducing agent in the reaction between acidified potassium manganate(VII) and potassium iodide solutions represented by the balanced equation below. Use your knowledge of the colours of the reactants and products to predict the colour change you would expect to see if you carried out this reaction. (9)

$$2MnO_4^- \ + \ 10I^- \ + \ 16H^+ \ \longrightarrow \ 2Mn^{2+} \ + \ 5I_2 \ + \ 8H_2O$$

(c) The chart compares the boiling points of alkanes and primary alcohols containing from one to four carbon atoms.

   (i) Give **two** reasons why each of these alcohols has a higher boiling point than the corresponding alkane. (7)

   (ii) Explain why the difference in boiling points between methane and methanol is 226.5 K while the difference in boiling points between butane and butanol is only 119 K. (6)

   (iii) Describe, in general terms, the solubilities of methane, methanol, butane and butanol in water. (12)

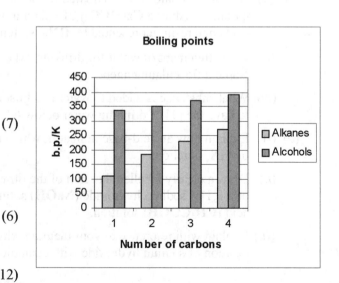

11. Answer any **two** of the parts (*a*), (*b*) and (*c*) (2×25)

(*a*) (*i*) What is an *ideal gas*? (4)

(*ii*) Give **one** reason why a real gas like carbon dioxide deviates from ideal behaviour. (3)

(*iii*) Assuming ideal behaviour, how many moles of carbon dioxide are present in 720 cm^3 of the gas at 10 °C and a pressure of 1×10^5 Pa? Give your answer correct to one significant figure. (9)

(*iv*) How many molecules of carbon dioxide are present in this quantity of carbon dioxide? (3)

(*v*) The reaction between carbon dioxide and limewater is represented by the following balanced equation.

$$Ca(OH)_2 \quad + \quad CO_2 \quad \longrightarrow \quad CaCO_3 \quad + \quad H_2O$$

What mass of calcium hydroxide is required to react completely with the quantity of carbon dioxide gas given in (*iii*) above? (6)

(*b*) State *Le Châtelier's principle*. (7)

The following equilibrium is set up in solution by dissolving cobalt(II) chloride crystals in water to form the pink species $Co(H_2O)_6^{2+}$ and then adding concentrated hydrochloric acid until the solution becomes blue.

$$\underset{\textbf{pink}}{Co(H_2O)_6^{2+}} \quad + \quad 4Cl^- \quad \rightleftharpoons \quad \underset{\textbf{blue}}{CoCl_4^{2-}} \quad + \quad 6H_2O$$

(*i*) When the solution becomes blue, has reaction ceased? Explain. (6)

(*ii*) The forward reaction is endothermic. State and explain the colour change observed on cooling the reaction mixture. (6)

(*iii*) Other than heating, mention **one** way of reversing the change caused by cooling the reaction mixture. (6)

(*c*) Answer part **A** *or* part **B**

A

Select **one** of the manufacturing processes below and answer the questions which follow:

ammonia manufacture   **nitric acid manufacture**   **magnesium oxide manufacture**

(*i*) What are the raw materials for the manufacturing process you have chosen? Describe how the raw materials are treated before they become the feedstock for the manufacturing process. (12)

(*ii*) Name **one** product of the process you have chosen, which, if discharged, could cause pollution. (3)

(*iii*) State the most important use of the *main* product of the process you have chosen. What makes this product particularly suitable for this use? (10)

or

B

A blast furnace may be used in the extraction of iron from iron ore.

(*i*) What materials must be added to a blast furnace in operation? (12)

(*ii*) Name the principal reducing agent in the blast furnace and write a balanced equation for its reaction with haematite (Fe_2O_3). (9)

(*iii*) Why is the pig iron produced in a blast furnace further processed into steel? (4)

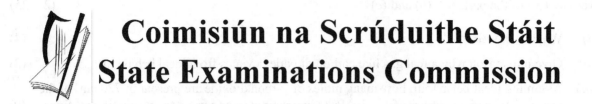

Coimisiún na Scrúduithe Stáit
State Examinations Commission

LEAVING CERTIFICATE EXAMINATION, 2005

CHEMISTRY - HIGHER LEVEL

TUESDAY, 21 JUNE – AFTERNOON 2.00 TO 5.00

---

400 MARKS

Answer **eight** questions in all

These **must** include at least **two** questions from **Section A**

All questions carry equal marks (50)

Information

Relative atomic masses: H = 1, C = 12, O = 16, Na = 23, Mg = 24, Cl = 35.5, Cr = 52, Cu = 63.5

Molar volume at room temperature and pressure = 24.0 litres

Avogadro constant = 6×10^{23} mol^{-1}

Universal gas constant, $R = 8.3$ $J\,K^{-1}\,mol^{-1}$

Section A

Answer at least <u>two</u> questions from this section [see page 1 for full instructions].

1. In an experiment to measure the concentration of dissolved oxygen in a river water sample, a bottle of water was filled from the river and it was analysed immediately. The experiment was carried out as follows:

    A few cm^3 each of concentrated manganese(II) sulfate (**MnSO$_4$**) solution and alkaline potassium iodide (**KOH/KI**) solution were added to the water in the bottle. The stopper was carefully replaced on the bottle and the bottle was shaken to ensure mixing of the reagents with the water. A brownish precipitate was produced. The stopper was removed from the bottle and a few cm^3 of concentrated sulfuric acid (**H$_2$SO$_4$**) were added carefully down the inside of the neck of the bottle using a dropper. The precipitate dissolved and a golden-brown solution was produced. The concentration of iodine (**I$_2$**) in this solution was found by titrating it in 50 cm^3 portions against a standard (0.01 M) sodium thiosulfate (**Na$_2$S$_2$O$_3$**) solution.

    (a) Why was it necessary to analyse the sample of river water *immediately*? (5)

    (b) In making the additions to the sample, why should the solutions used be *concentrated*? (6)

    (c) Describe how the additions of the concentrated solution of manganese(II) sulfate (**MnSO$_4$**) and alkaline potassium iodide (**KOH/KI**) to the bottle of river water should be carried out. What essential precaution should be taken when replacing the stopper of the bottle after these additions are made? (9)

    (d) Describe clearly the procedure for using a pipette to measure exactly 50 cm^3 portions of the iodine (**I$_2$**) solution into the titration flask. (9)

    (e) What indicator is used in this titration? State when the indicator should be added to the titration flask and describe the colour change observed at the end point. (9)

    (f) The titration reaction is described by the following equation.

    $$2S_2O_3^{2-} \quad + \quad I_2 \quad \rightarrow \quad 2I^- \quad + \quad S_4O_6^{2-}$$

    Calculate the concentration of the iodine solution in moles per litre given that 6.0 cm^3 of the 0.01 M sodium thiosulfate (**Na$_2$S$_2$O$_3$**) solution were required in the titration for complete reaction with 50 cm^3 portions of the iodine solution. (6)

    (g) For every 1 mole of oxygen gas (**O$_2$**) in the water sample 2 moles of iodine (**I$_2$**) are liberated in this experiment. Hence calculate the concentration of dissolved oxygen in the water sample in p.p.m. (6)

2. A group of students prepared ethanal (CH_3CHO) by slowly adding an aqueous solution of ethanol (C_2H_5OH) and sodium dichromate(VI) ($Na_2Cr_2O_7.2H_2O$) to a hot aqueous solution of sulfuric acid (H_2SO_4). The apparatus drawn below was used. The reaction is described by the following equation.

$$3C_2H_5OH + Cr_2O_7^{2-} + 8H^+ \rightarrow 3CH_3CHO + 2Cr^{3+} + 7H_2O$$

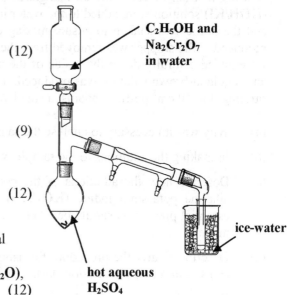

(a) Why was the receiving vessel cooled in ice-water? (5)

(b) State **two** features of the preparation that are necessary to maximise the yield of ethanal <u>and</u>, for each feature stated, explain why it is necessary. (12)

(c) Describe <u>and</u> account for the colour change which is observed during the addition of the ethanol and sodium dichromate(VI) solution to the hot acid. (9)

(d) Describe how you would carry out Fehling's test on a sample of ethanal. What observation would you expect to make in this test? (12)

(e) Assuming that all of the features needed to maximise the yield of ethanal were present, what mass of ethanal would be produced in the preparation if the students used 8.94 g of sodium dichromate(VI) ($Na_2Cr_2O_7.2H_2O$), and a 75% yield was obtained? (12)

---

3. Hydrogen peroxide decomposes rapidly in the presence of a manganese(IV) oxide (MnO_2) catalyst.

(a) Write a balanced equation for the decomposition of hydrogen peroxide. (5)

(b) Draw a labelled diagram of an apparatus a student could assemble to measure the rate of decomposition of hydrogen peroxide in the presence of a manganese(IV) oxide (MnO_2) catalyst. Indicate clearly how the reaction could be started at a time known exactly, and how the gas produced is collected and its volume measured. (12)

(c) A student has a choice of using the same mass of finely powdered manganese(IV) oxide or coarsely powdered (granulated) manganese(IV) oxide. Which of these would you expect to have a greater average rate of reaction over the first minute of the reaction? Give a reason for your answer. (6)

A set of results obtained in an experiment to measure the rate of decomposition of hydrogen peroxide, in a solution of known volume and concentration, is given in the table.

Time/minutes	0	1	2	3	4	5	6	7	8
Volume of O_2/cm^3	0.0	13.5	23.4	30.5	35.4	38.3	39.6	40.0	40.0

(d) Plot a graph to illustrate the volume of oxygen produced *versus* time. (12)

(e) Use the graph to determine
   (i) the volume of oxygen produced during the first 2.5 minutes and
   (ii) the instantaneous rate of the reaction at 2.5 minutes. (9)

(f) What changes would you expect in the graph if the experiment were repeated using a solution of the same volume but exactly half the concentration of the original hydrogen peroxide solution? (6)

Section B

[See page 1 for instructions regarding the number of questions to be answered]

4. Answer **eight** of the following items (*a*), (*b*), (*c*), etc. (50)

   (*a*) Define *electronegativity*.

   (*b*) What are the possible shapes for molecules of general formula AB_2?

   (*c*) Name the series of coloured lines in the line emission spectrum of hydrogen corresponding to transitions of electrons from higher energy levels to the second (n = 2) energy level.

   (*d*) What contribution did Dobereiner make to the systematic arrangement of the elements?

   (*e*) Distinguish between an *atomic orbital* and a *sub-level*.

   (*f*) How could you confirm the presence of nitrate ions in an aqueous solution?

   (*g*) Name <u>and</u> draw the structure of an aromatic compound of molecular formula C_8H_{10}.

   (*h*) When 3.175 g of copper reacts with chlorine gas 6.725 g of copper chloride is formed. Find by calculation the empirical formula of the chloride.

   (*i*) Draw the structural formula of an organic compound of molecular formula C_3H_6. Label clearly any tetrahedrally bonded carbon atom in the molecule.

   (*j*) Complete and balance the following equation:

   $$C_2H_5OH \quad + \quad Na \quad \rightarrow$$

   (*k*) Answer part **A** <u>or</u> **B**.

   A Describe using chemical equations the chain reaction process whereby chlorine free radicals break down ozone in the stratosphere.

   or

   B How does a sacrificial anode protect a metal from corrosion?

   _____

5. (*a*) What are *isotopes*? (5)

   Name the scientist pictured on the right who is credited with the discovery in 1896 that uranium salts emit radiation. (3)

   Give an example of a radioactive isotope and state **one** common use made of this isotope. (9)

   (*b*) Define *atomic radius (covalent radius)*. (6)

   Describe and account for the trend in atomic radii (covalent radii) of the elements

   (*i*) across the second period, (*ii*) down any group, of the periodic table. (15)

   (*c*) Define *covalent bond*. (6)
   Distinguish between a sigma (σ) and a pi (π) covalent bond. (6)

6. (*a*) The octane number of a fuel is described as *a measure of the tendency of the fuel to cause knocking*, or as *a measure of the tendency of the fuel to resist auto-ignition*. This number is found by comparing the combustion of the fuel with the combustion of a mixture of two reference hydrocarbons using the same standard engine.

   (*i*) Name **both** of the reference hydrocarbons present in the mixture used when measuring octane number by this comparison method. (8)

   (*ii*) State **two** structural features of a hydrocarbon molecule which contribute to it having a high octane number. (6)

   (*iii*) Lead compounds were used in the past to increase the octane number of fuels. Why are lead compounds unsuitable as additives for petrol used in modern cars? (3)

   (*iv*) Identify **one** additive *or* type of additive, other than a compound of lead, used to increase the octane number of fuels. (3)

(*b*) There are **three** structural isomers of the hydrocarbon of formula C_5H_{12}. In the case of **each** of these isomers, draw the structure of the molecule <u>and</u> give its systematic IUPAC name. (18)

(*c*) The combustion of liquid benzene is described by the following equation:

$$2C_6H_{6(l)} \quad + \quad 15O_{2(g)} \quad \rightarrow \quad 12CO_{2(g)} \quad + \quad 6H_2O_{(l)}$$

Given that the heats of formation of carbon dioxide gas, liquid water and liquid benzene are -394, -286 and 49 kJ mol^{-1} respectively, calculate the heat of combustion of liquid benzene. (12)

---

7. Examine the reaction scheme and answer the questions which follow.

$$C_2H_5OH \xrightarrow{\ \ W\ \ } C_2H_4 \xrightarrow{\ \ X\ \ } C_2H_6$$

with Y and Z leading to

$$C_2H_5Cl$$
$$\underline{A}$$

(*a*) Name the compound labelled **<u>A</u>**. (5)

(*b*) For each of the conversions **W, X, Y** and **Z**, classify it as an *addition*, an *elimination* or a *substitution* reaction. (12)

(*c*) Describe with the aid of a labelled diagram how the conversion **W** may be carried out in a school laboratory and how a sample of the product may be collected. How would you test this product to show that it is unsaturated? (18)

(*d*) The conversion labelled **Z** is known to occur by a *free radical* mechanism.
State **three** clear pieces of experimental evidence which support this mechanism. (15)

---

8. (*a*) Define (i) *acid*, (ii) *base*, according to the Brønsted-Lowry theory. (8)

(*b*) Identify **one** species acting as an acid, and also identify its conjugate base, in the following system.

$$H_2F^+ \quad + \quad Cl^- \quad \rightleftharpoons \quad HCl \quad + \quad HF \tag{6}$$

(*c*) Calculate the pH of a 0.002 M solution of methanoic acid (**HCOOH**).
The value of K_a for methanoic acid is 1.8×10^{-4}. (12)

(*d*) What is meant by the *biochemical oxygen demand* (*BOD*) of a water sample? (6)

(*e*) Describe clearly the processes involved in the primary and secondary stages of urban sewage treatment. What substances are removed by tertiary treatment of sewage? (18)

9. (a) State *Le Chatelier's principle.* (5)

(b) A student is provided with glassware and other laboratory apparatus as well as the following chemicals: potassium dichromate(VI) ($K_2Cr_2O_7.2H_2O$), hydrochloric acid ($HCl_{(aq)}$), sodium hydroxide (NaOH), cobalt(II) chloride crystals ($CoCl_2.6H_2O$) and deionised water (H_2O).

   (i) Describe clearly how the student could use a selection of the chemicals listed above to establish a chemical equilibrium. Write a balanced equation for the equilibrium. (12)

   (ii) Describe how the student could then demonstrate the effect of concentration on that chemical equilibrium. State the observations made during the demonstration. (9)

(c) The value of K_c for the following equilibrium reaction is 4.0 at a temperature of 373 K.

$$CH_3COOH + C_2H_5OH \rightleftharpoons CH_3COOC_2H_5 + H_2O$$

   (i) Write the equilibrium constant (K_c) expression for this reaction. (6)

   (ii) What mass of ethyl ethanoate ($CH_3COOC_2H_5$) would be present in the equilibrium mixture if 15 g of ethanoic acid and 11.5 g of ethanol were mixed and equilibrium was established at this temperature? (18)

---

10. Answer any **two** of the parts (a), (b) and (c). (2×25)

(a) An indigestion tablet contains a mass of 0.30 g of magnesium hydroxide [$Mg(OH)_2$] as its only basic ingredient. The balanced chemical equation for the reaction between magnesium hydroxide and hydrochloric acid ($HCl_{(aq)}$), the acid produced in the stomach, is as follows:

$$Mg(OH)_2 + 2HCl \longrightarrow MgCl_2 + 2H_2O$$

   (i) Calculate the volume of 1.0 M **HCl** neutralised by <u>two</u> of these indigestion tablets. Give your answer correct to the nearest cm^3. (8)

   (ii) What mass of salt is formed in this neutralisation? (5)

   (iii) How many magnesium ions are present in this amount of the salt? (6)

   (iv) Another indigestion remedy consists of a suspension of magnesium hydroxide [$Mg(OH)_2$] in water and is marked 6% (w/v).
   What volume of this second indigestion remedy would have the same neutralising effect on stomach acid as two of the indigestion tablets mentioned earlier? (6)

(b) *The minimum energy required to completely remove the most loosely bound electron from a mole of gaseous atoms in their ground state* defines an important property of every element.

   (i) Identify the energy quantity defined above. State the unit used to measure this quantity. (7)

   (ii) Using **X** to represent an element, express the definition above in the form of a balanced chemical equation. (6)

   (iii) Would it take more or less energy to remove the most loosely bound electron from an atom if that electron were not in its ground state? Explain. (6)

   (iv) An element has a low first ionisation energy value and a low electronegativity value. What does this information tell you about how reactive the element is likely to be, and what is likely to happen to the atoms of the element when they react? (6)

(c) State the principle on which all chromatographic separation techniques are based. (10)

   Describe with the aid of clearly labelled diagrams how you could carry out an experiment to separate a mixture of dyes (or indicators) using paper, thin-layer or column chromatography. (15)

37

11. Answer any **two** of the parts (*a*), (*b*) and (*c*).   (2 × 25)

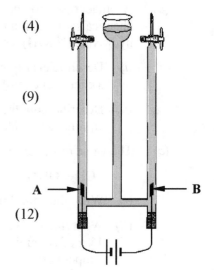

(*a*) (*i*)   Define *oxidation* in terms of change in oxidation number.   (4)

(*ii*)   What is observed when chlorine gas is bubbled into an aqueous solution of sodium bromide?

Explain your answer in terms of oxidation and reduction.   (9)

(*iii*)   A solution of acidified water (dilute sulfuric acid) is electrolysed by passing an electric current through it using inert electrodes. At which electrode **A** or **B** does oxidation occur? Which species is oxidised? Write a balanced half equation for the oxidation reaction.   (12)

(*b*) (*i*)   Define *a mole of a substance*.   (7)

(*ii*)   State *Avogadro's law*.   (6)

(*iii*)   A foil balloon has a capacity of 10 litres. How many atoms of helium occupy this balloon when it is filled with a 10% (v/v) mixture of helium in air at room temperature and pressure?   (12)

(*c*) Answer either part **A** *or* part **B**.

A

(*i*)   What is meant by the term *addition polymerisation*?   (7)

(*ii*)   Name the Du Pont chemist pictured on the right who discovered poly(tetrafluoroethene), PTFE.   (3)

(*iii*)   Describe using an equation how poly(tetrafluoroethene) is produced from its monomers.   (9)

(*iv*)   Give **two** common uses of PTFE.   (6)

Discoverer of PTFE

or

B

(*i*)   Account for the inert nature of nitrogen gas.   (7)

(*ii*)   What is meant by *nitrogen fixation*?

State **two** ways by which nitrogen is fixed in nature.   (9)

(*iii*)   The concentration of **NO_2** in the atmosphere has increased in the past fifty years. Describe with the aid of chemical equations how an increase in the number of cars has contributed to this change.   (9)

Coimisiún na Scrúduithe Stáit
State Examinations Commission

LEAVING CERTIFICATE EXAMINATION, 2004

CHEMISTRY - HIGHER LEVEL

TUESDAY, 22 JUNE – AFTERNOON 2.00 TO 5.00

400 MARKS

Answer **eight** questions in all

These **must** include at least **two** questions from **Section A**

All questions carry equal marks (50)

Information

Relative atomic masses: H = 1, C = 12, O = 16, Na = 23, Cl = 35.5, Ca = 40, Fe = 56.

Molar volume at room temperature and pressure = 24.0 litres

Universal gas constant, $R = 8.3$ J K^{-1} mol^{-1}

Section A

Answer at least two questions from this section [see page 1 for full instructions].

1. In an experiment to determine the total hardness of a water sample containing both calcium and magnesium ions, a solution of the reagent **edta** (ethylenediaminetetraacetic acid) in the form of its disodium salt (represented by Na_2H_2Y) was titrated against a sample of the water using a suitable indicator. The reaction between the ions (represented by M^{2+}) in the hard water and the **edta** reagent may be represented as

$$M^{2+} \quad + \quad H_2Y^{2-} \quad \longrightarrow \quad MY^{2-} \quad + \quad 2H^+$$

(a) Name a suitable indicator for this titration.
What colour change is observed at the end point of the titration using this indicator? (8)

(b) Describe the correct procedure for rinsing the burette and filling it with **edta** reagent. (15)

(c) The addition of a small quantity of another solution to the water in the conical flask is essential before commencing the titration. What solution must be added and what is its purpose? (6)

(d) In the experiment it was found that 100 cm³ portions of the water required an average titre of 8.10 cm³ of 0.010 M **edta** solution. Calculate the total hardness in
  (i)   moles per litre,
  (ii) grams per litre expressed in terms of $CaCO_3$ and
  (iii) p.p.m. expressed in terms of $CaCO_3$. (15)

(e) A whitish deposit is often found on the insides of kettles in hard water districts. If some of this deposit is scraped into a test tube and dilute hydrochloric acid is added a reaction is observed. Write a balanced equation for this reaction. (6)

---

2. The diagram shows the experimental set-up used by a group of students to prepare a sample of ethene from ethanol and to collect the ethene produced.

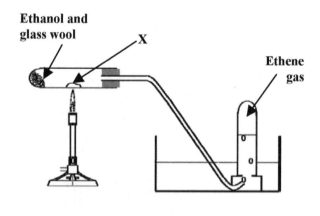

(a) What is the function of the glass wool? (5)
Identify the solid **X** and describe its appearance. (6)

(b) State and explain **two** safety precautions which should be observed when carrying out the student experiment. (12)

(c) Write a balanced equation for the reaction involved in this preparation. (6)

(d) If the ethene produced is bubbled through an acidified solution of potassium manganate(VII), the solution is decolorised showing that ethene is *unsaturated*. What is meant by the term *unsaturated*? Describe how you would carry out another test to confirm that ethene is unsaturated. (12)

(e) Describe the flame that would be observed when a combustion test is carried out on a sample of ethene gas. Write a balanced equation for the combustion of ethene in excess oxygen. (9)

---

3. (a) A sample of impure benzoic acid was recrystallised as follows: 2.5 g of the impure benzoic acid was weighed out and dissolved in the minimum amount of hot water. The hot solution was filtered and the filtrate was allowed to cool and recrystallise. The recrystallised benzoic acid was isolated by filtration. After drying, 2.25 g of purified acid were obtained.

   (i) Why is it important to use the minimum amount of hot water in the procedure? (5)

   (ii) Indicate clearly the stage of the recrystallisation procedure at which *insoluble* impurities were removed and how their removal was achieved. Indicate also the stage at which *soluble* impurities were removed and how their removal was achieved. (12)

   (iii) How could you have ensured that the recrystallisation was complete? (3)

   (iv) How could the crystals have been dried? (3)

   (v) What was the percentage yield of purified benzoic acid? (3)

   (b) Melting points of samples of the impure and recrystallised benzoic acid were taken and compared.

   (i) Describe with the aid of a labelled diagram how you would have measured the melting point of one of these samples. (15)

   (ii) Give **two** ways in which you would expect the melting point of the impure benzoic acid to differ from that of the purified acid. (6)

   (iii) State **one** use of benzoic acid and its salts. (3)

Section B

[See page 1 for instructions regarding the number of questions to be answered]

4. Answer **eight** of the following items (*a*), (*b*), (*c*), etc. (50)

   (*a*) Define *relative atomic mass*.

   (*b*) Account for the difference in the shapes of the ammonia (NH_3) and boron trifluoride (BF_3) molecules.

   (*c*) The boiling points of hydrogen and oxygen are 20.0 K and 90.2 K respectively. Account for the higher boiling point of oxygen.

   (*d*) State *Charles' law*.

   (*e*) Write (*i*) the conjugate acid and (*ii*) the conjugate base of HPO_4^{2-}.

   (*f*) How are heavy metals, e.g. mercury, removed from industrial waste before it is discharged into rivers, lakes or the sea?

   (*g*) What is the oxidation number (*i*) of oxygen in H_2O_2 and (*ii*) of bromine in $KBrO_3$?

   (*h*) What is the percentage by mass of iron in iron(III) oxide (Fe_2O_3)?

   (*i*) State <u>and</u> explain the colour observed at the negative electrode in the electrolysis of aqueous potassium iodide, containing a little phenolphthalein indicator, using inert electrodes.

   (*j*) How could the presence of sulfite ions in aqueous solution be detected?

   (*k*) Answer part **A** <u>or</u> **B**.

   A   How is oxygen gas produced industrially?

   or

   B   How does the anodising of aluminium protect it from corrosion?

   _____

5. (*a*) Write the electron configuration (*s*, *p*, etc.) of the nitrogen atom. (5)

   Show, using dot and cross diagrams, the bond formation in a nitrogen molecule.
   Describe the bonding in the nitrogen molecule in terms of sigma (σ) and pi (π) bonding. (9)

   What type of intermolecular forces would you expect to find in nitrogen gas? Explain your answer. (6)

   (*b*) Define *first ionisation energy*. (9)

   There is a general increase in first ionisation energy across a period of the periodic table.
   State the **two** principal reasons for this trend. (6)

   The table shows the first and second ionisation energies of nitrogen, oxygen, neon and sodium.

   Account for the decrease in first ionisation energy between nitrogen and oxygen.

   Explain why the second ionisation energy of sodium is significantly (about nine times) higher than the first while the increase in the second ionisation energy of neon compared to its first is relatively small (less than twice the first). (15)

Element	First ionisation energy (kJ mol^{-1})	Second ionisation energy (kJ mol^{-1})
Nitrogen	1400	2860
Oxygen	1310	3390
Neon	2080	3950
Sodium	494	4560

_____

6. (a) Define (i) *heat of formation of a substance,* (ii) *octane number of a fuel.* (11)

(b) The combustion of methane is described by the following balanced equation.

$$CH_{4(g)} + 2O_{2(g)} \longrightarrow CO_{2(g)} + 2H_2O_{(l)} \qquad \Delta H = -890.4 \text{ kJ mol}^{-1}$$

The standard heats of formation of carbon dioxide and water are –394 and –286 kJ mol^{-1} respectively. Calculate the heat of formation of methane. (12)

(c) Methane is an excellent fuel. Give **two** properties of methane which account for its usefulness as a fuel. Natural gas is a rich source of methane. Why are mercaptans often added to natural gas? (9)

(d) Methane is often found in gas fields which occur in association with crude oil deposits. Crude oil is fractionated in order to obtain more useful products. Outline clearly how the fractionation process is carried out. (12)

(e) Identify **two** structural features of a hydrocarbon fuel which affect its octane number. (6)

_____

7. (a) Copy into your answer book the structure of the ester shown and indicate clearly on your diagram a carbon atom which is in planar geometry in the molecule, and also a carbon atom which is in tetrahedral geometry in the molecule. (8)

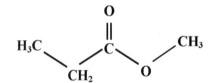

(b) Give the names of the alcohol <u>and</u> of the carboxylic acid from which the ester shown in the diagram is synthesised. What organic reaction type describes this esterification reaction? (15)

(c) The carboxylic acid you were asked to name in (b) may itself be synthesised in two steps from an alcohol.

(i) Identify the alcohol from which the carboxylic acid is derived.
(ii) Give the name <u>and</u> structure of the intermediate organic compound in this synthesis.
(iii) Identify the type of organic reaction involved in each step.
(iv) Identify the inorganic reagents which may be used in this synthesis. (21)

(d) State **two** common uses of esters. (6)

_____

8. (a) Define the *rate of a chemical reaction.* (5)

Explain why increasing the temperature has a significant effect on the rate of a reaction. (6)

(b) The diagram shows a reaction profile diagram for an endothermic reaction. Name the quantities of energy marked **A** and **B**.

Copy this diagram into your answer book and indicate clearly on your diagram the likely effect of adding a catalyst on the energy profile for the reaction. (12)

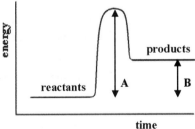

(c) Catalytic converters are fitted to all modern cars with petrol engines. Name **two** elements used as catalysts in a catalytic converter. Name **one** substance which poisons the catalysts in a catalytic converter. (9)

(d) The oxidation of potassium sodium tartrate by hydrogen peroxide catalysed by cobalt(II) ions provides evidence for the intermediate formation theory of catalysis. State the observations you would make when carrying out this experiment. Explain how these observations provide evidence for the intermediate formation theory. (18)

_____

43

9. (a) What is meant by *chemical equilibrium*? Why is it described as a *dynamic* state? (8)

Consider the following reversible chemical reaction:

$$N_{2(g)} \quad + \quad 3H_{2(g)} \quad \rightleftharpoons \quad 2NH_{3(g)} \quad \Delta H \ = \ -92.4 \, kJ$$

(b) Use Le Chatelier's principle to predict the levels (high or low) of temperature and pressure needed to maximise the yield of ammonia when equilibrium is established. Give a reason (*i*) for the temperature level you have predicted, (*ii*) for the level of pressure you have predicted. (12)

(c) Are the temperature levels predicted using Le Chatelier's principle actually used to maximise ammonia yield in industry? Explain your answer. (6)

(d) What is the effect of a catalyst on a reversible reaction? (6)

(e) In an experiment 6.0 moles of nitrogen and 18.0 moles of hydrogen were mixed and allowed to come to equilibrium in a sealed 5.0 litre vessel at a certain temperature. It was found that there were 6.0 moles of ammonia in the equilibrium mixture.
Write the equilibrium constant expression for the reaction and calculate the value of the equilibrium constant (K_c) at this temperature. (18)

---

10. Answer any **two** of the parts (*a*), (*b*) and (*c*). (2 × 25)

(a) Hydrochloric acid is severely corrosive to skin and eyes and toxic by inhalation or ingestion. It should be handled carefully and stored safely.

The entire contents of a bottle containing 2.5 litres of concentrated hydrochloric acid were accidentally spilled in a laboratory. The spilled acid was neutralised by adding solid powdered sodium carbonate. The neutralisation reaction is described by the following equation.

$$Na_2CO_3 \quad + \quad 2HCl \quad \longrightarrow \quad 2NaCl \quad + \quad H_2O \quad + \quad CO_2$$

The spilled acid was a 36% (w/v) solution of hydrogen chloride in water.

(*i*) Calculate the number of moles of hydrochloric acid spilled. (10)

(*ii*) What was the minimum mass of anhydrous sodium carbonate required to completely neutralise all of the spilled hydrochloric acid? (9)

(*iii*) What volume of carbon dioxide in litres, at room temperature and pressure, was produced in this neutralisation reaction? (6)

(b) Describe how Bohr used line emission spectra to explain the existence of energy levels in atoms. (13)

(*i*) Why does each element have a unique line emission spectrum? (6)

(*ii*) The fact that each element has a unique line spectrum forms the basis for an instrumental technique which can be used to detect heavy metals and to measure their concentrations in a soil or a water sample. Name the instrumental technique. (3)

(*iii*) Bohr's atomic theory was later modified. Give **one** reason why this theory was updated. (3)

(c) State *Avogadro's law*. (5)

(*i*) What is an ideal gas? (5)

(*ii*) State **one** reason why ammonia gas deviates from ideal gas behaviour. (3)

(*iii*) A small quantity of the volatile organic solvent propanone (C_3H_6O) evaporates at room temperature and pressure. Use the equation of state for an ideal gas to calculate the volume, in litres, of propanone vapour formed when 0.29 g of liquid propanone evaporates taking room temperature as 20 °C and room pressure as 101 kPa. (12)

---

11. Answer any **two** of the parts (*a*), (*b*) and (*c*).   (2 × 25)

(*a*) Define radioactivity.   (6)

   (*i*)   State **two** properties of beta (β) particles.   (6)

   (*ii*) Write an equation for the nuclear reaction involved in the beta decay of ^{14}C (carbon-14).   (6)

   (*iii*) Explain how the carbon-14 isotope allows certain archaeological discoveries to be dated.   (7)

(*b*) Define pH.   (7)

   (*i*)   What are the limitations of the pH scale?   (6)

   (*ii*) Calculate the approximate pH of a vinegar solution that contains 4.5 g of ethanoic acid per 100 cm^3. The value of K_a for ethanoic acid is 1.8×10^{-5}.   (12)

(*c*) Answer either part **A** or part **B**.

   A

   Write a brief note on the contribution made to our understanding of crystal structures by
   (*i*)   Lawrence and William Bragg,
   (*ii*) Dorothy Hodgkin.   (7)

Lawrence and William Bragg

   What type of crystal is formed by iodine <u>and</u> what are the binding forces in the crystal?   (6)

   Explain
   (*i*)   why metals are generally good conductors of electricity,
   (*ii*) why most ionic crystals dissolve in water.   (12)

Dorothy Hodgkin

or

   B

   The *greenhouse effect* is a natural phenomenon but its effects have been enhanced by human activity over the past 200 years.

   (*i*)   Explain the term *greenhouse effect*.   (7)

   (*ii*) Identify **one** gas in the atmosphere which makes a significant contribution to the greenhouse effect.   (3)

   (*iii*) In relation to the gas you have identified in (*ii*), mention a type of human activity which has been a major contributor to the increased levels of this gas in the atmosphere.   (3)

   (*iv*) Identify **one** gas, found in the atmosphere, which is not a greenhouse gas.   (3)

   (*v*)   State **three** probable consequences of an increased greenhouse effect which have been suggested by environmental scientists.   (9)

Coimisiún na Scrúduithe Stáit
State Examinations Commission

LEAVING CERTIFICATE EXAMINATION, 2003

CHEMISTRY - HIGHER LEVEL

TUESDAY, 17 JUNE - AFTERNOON 2.00 to 5.00

---

400 MARKS

Answer **eight** questions in all

These **must** include at least **two** questions from **Section A**

All questions carry equal marks (50)

Information

Relative atomic masses: H = 1, C = 12, N = 14, O = 16, Na = 23, Fe = 56.

Molar volume at s.t.p. = 22.4 l

Avogadro constant = 6×10^{23} mol^{-1}

Universal gas constant, $R = 8.3$ J K^{-1} mol^{-1}

Section A

Answer at least <u>two</u> questions from this section [see page 1 for full instructions]

1. Iron tablets may be used in the treatment of anaemia.

    To analyse the iron(II) content of commercially available iron tablets a student used four tablets, each of mass 0.360 g, to make up 250 cm^3 of solution in a volumetric flask using dilute sulfuric acid and deionised water.

    About 15 cm^3 of dilute sulfuric acid was added to 25 cm^3 portions of this iron(II) solution and the mixture then titrated with a 0.010 M solution of potassium manganate(VII), **KMnO$_4$**.

    (a) Why was it important to use dilute sulfuric acid as well as deionised water in making up the solution from the tablets? (5)

    (b) Describe in detail the procedure for making up the 250 cm^3 solution from the tablets. (18)

    (c) Why was more dilute sulfuric acid added before the titrations were commenced? (6)

    (d) How was the end-point detected? (3)

    The titration reaction is described by the equation

    $$MnO_4^- \; + \; 5Fe^{2+} \; + \; 8H^+ \; \longrightarrow \; Mn^{2+} \; + \; 5Fe^{3+} \; + \; 4H_2O$$

    (e) In the titrations the 25 cm^3 portions of the iron(II) solution made from the tablets required 13.9 cm^3 of the 0.010 M **KMnO$_4$** solution. Calculate

        (i) the concentration of the iron(II) solution in moles per litre

        (ii) the mass of iron(II) in one tablet

        (iii) the percentage by mass of iron(II) in each tablet. (18)

---

2. The diagram shows an apparatus that can be used for the preparation of ethyne gas, C_2H_2.

A liquid **X** is dropped onto the solid **Y** and the gas collected in test tubes as shown.

(a) Identify the liquid **X** and the solid **Y**.　(8)

(b) Describe the appearance of the solid **Y**.　(3)

(c) Write a balanced equation for the reaction between **X** and **Y** producing ethyne.　(6)

(d) What is observed when a sample of ethyne gas is burned in air?
Write a balanced equation for the combustion of ethyne in oxygen.　(9)

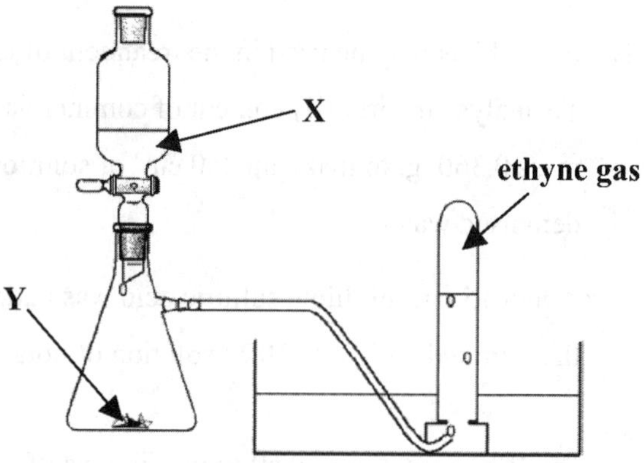

(e) Ethyne, C_2H_2, is described as an *unsaturated* hydrocarbon.

Describe a test you could carry out to show that ethyne is *unsaturated*.
Write an equation for the reaction taking place. Name the organic product.　(18)

(f) The common name for ethyne gas, C_2H_2, is acetylene. Give **one** major use of the gas.　(6)

———————————————

3. In an experiment to determine the relative molecular mass of a volatile liquid a sample of the liquid is vaporised at a given temperature and pressure and its volume measured. The mass of the sample is also measured. The number of moles of liquid is then calculated using the formula $PV = nRT$ and from this the relative molecular mass of the liquid is calculated.

(a) What is meant by a *volatile liquid*?　(5)

(b) Describe with the aid of a labelled diagram how you would carry out this experiment to determine the relative molecular mass of a volatile liquid. From your description it should be clear how the *mass*, *volume*, and *temperature*, of the sample are measured.　(21)

(c) How may the *pressure* be measured?　(6)

In an experiment to measure the relative molecular mass of a volatile liquid 0.275 g of the liquid was vaporised at 97 °C. The volume occupied was found to be 95 cm^3. The pressure was 1×10^5 Pa.

(d) Calculate the number of moles of the volatile liquid vaporised.　(12)

(e) Calculate the relative molecular mass of the volatile liquid.　(6)

———————————————

48

Section B

[See page 1 for instructions regarding the number of questions to be answered]

4. Answer **eight** of the following items (a), (b), (c), etc. (50)

(a) How many (i) electrons and (ii) neutrons has $^{37}_{17}Cl^-$?

(b) How many electrons are there in 2.3 g of sodium metal, **Na**?

(c) The famous Irish scientist shown on the right, was born in 1627. He was a son of the Earl of Cork. Give a statement of the gas law that bears his name.

(d) On what principle is the analytical technique *mass spectrometry* based?

(e) What happens during *secondary* sewage treatment?

(f) List the following three types of radiation in order of <u>increasing</u> penetrating power

      alpha- (α-)   **beta- (β-)**   **gamma- (γ-)**

(g) What is the percentage by mass of nitrogen in ammonium nitrate, NH_4NO_3?

(h) Draw the structure <u>and</u> give the name of an *ester* of the molecular formula $C_3H_6O_2$.

(i) State **two** ways in which Mendeleev's periodic table of the elements differs from that of Moseley.

(j) State **two** ways, other than the addition of lead compounds, that the octane rating of a fuel can be increased.

(k) Answer part **A** <u>or</u> **B**

    A   Describe with the aid of an equation how *nitrogen fixation* occur in nature.

or

    B   State **two** properties of transition metals.

_____

5. (a) Define (i) *energy level*   (ii) *atomic orbital.* (8)

    (iii) Write the electronic configuration (*s, p,* etc.) of nitrogen.

    (iv) Describe how the electrons are arranged in the orbitals of the highest occupied sub-level of a nitrogen atom in its ground state. (6)

(b) Define *electronegativity*. (6)

    (i) Describe using dot and cross diagrams the bonding in the water molecule. (9)

    (ii) What is the shape of the water molecule?
        Which of the following angles, 104°, 107°, 109°, 120° or 180° would you expect to be closest to the bond angle in the water molecule? Explain your answer. (12)

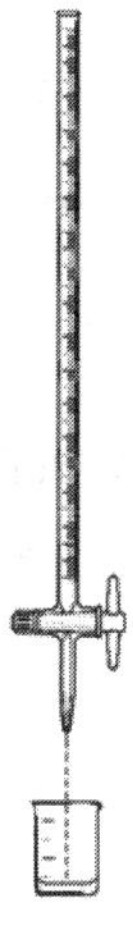

(c) The diagram on the right shows a thin stream of water flowing from a burette.

    What would you observe if a charged rod was brought close to the thin stream of water? Explain your answer. (9)

_____

6. Study the reaction scheme and answer the questions which follow.

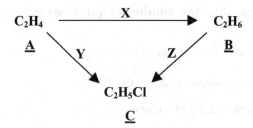

(a) Which of the compounds **A**, **B** and **C** has no tetrahedrally bonded carbon atoms?
Draw the structure of a molecule of this compound. (8)

(b) Classify the conversions **X**, **Y** and **Z** as *addition, substitution or elimination* reactions. (9)

(c) What reagent is used to convert **A** to **C**? (3)

(d) What reagent and what conditions are required for the conversion of **B** to **C**? (6)

(e) Describe the mechanism of the reaction for the conversion of **A** to **C**. (18)
State **one** piece of experimental evidence which supports the mechanism you have proposed. (6)

---

7. (a) Define *rate of a chemical reaction*. (5)

Calcium carbonate (marble chips) reacts with hydrochloric acid according to the following equation.

$$CaCO_3 \ + \ 2HCl \ \longrightarrow \ CaCl_2 \ + \ CO_2 \ + \ H_2O$$

Using simple experiments involving marble chips, $CaCO_3$, and hydrochloric acid, **HCl**, describe how you could demonstrate the effects of

(i) *particle size*, (ii) *concentration* on the rate of a chemical reaction. (18)

(b) What is a *catalyst*? (6)

Catalytic converters are used in cars.

(i) Identify **one** reaction which is catalysed in the catalytic converter in a car.
State **one** of the environmental benefits of this process. (12)

(ii) Name **one** element used as a catalyst in a catalytic converter.
What type of catalysis is involved in a catalytic converter? (9)

---

8. (a) Define (i) *an acid*, (ii) *a base* according to the Brønsted-Lowry theory. (8)

Identify the *acid*, and *conjugate acid* in the following system. (6)

$$H_2S \ + \ O^{2-} \ \rightleftharpoons \ OH^- \ + \ SH^-$$

(b) Define pH. (6)

A bottle of vinegar is labelled 6% (w/v) acetic acid (ethanoic acid). The dissociation constant, K_a, for ethanoic acid is 1.8×10^{-5}. Calculate the approximate pH of the vinegar solution. (12)

(c) The *free chlorine* present in swimming-pool water can be measured using a colorimeter or comparator.

(i) What is the principle on which the technique that uses each of these methods is based? (12)

(ii) What is meant by *free chlorine*? (6)

---

9. (*a*) Draw the structure and state the IUPAC name for the aldehyde of the molecular formula **C₃H₆O**. (8)

Draw the structure and give the name of another carbonyl compound that has the same molecular formula, **C₃H₆O**. Give **one** use of this compound. (12)

Which of these two carbonyl compounds is easily oxidised to a carboxylic acid? Name that acid. (6)

(*b*) The diagram shows the arrangement of glassware for the extraction of clove oil from cloves by steam distillation.

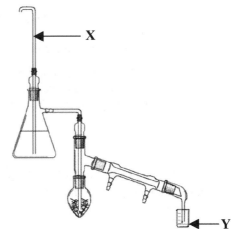

    (*i*)   What is the purpose of the tube marked **X**? (6)

    (*ii*)   What is collected at **Y**? Describe its appearance. (12)

    (*iii*) State **one** use of clove oil. (6)

_____

10. Answer any **two** of the parts (*a*), (*b*) or (*c*)   (2 × 25)

(*a*) Define *heat of combustion*. (7)

Propane may be used in gas cylinders for cooking appliances.
Propane burns according to the equation

$$C_3H_8 \quad + \quad 5O_2 \quad \longrightarrow \quad 3CO_2 \quad + \quad 4H_2O$$

    (*i*)   The heats of formation of propane, carbon dioxide and water are −104, −394 and −286 kJ mol⁻¹ respectively. Calculate the heat of combustion of propane. (12)

    (*ii*)   If 500 kJ of energy are needed to boil a kettle of water what mass of propane gas must be burned to generate this amount of heat? Express your answer to the nearest gram. (6)

(*b*) Use the data below to sketch (on graph paper) the pH curve for a titration between 20 cm³ of ethanoic acid and a sodium hydroxide solution added from a burette. (18)

Volume of NaOH added (cm³)	0	5	10	15	17	19	21	23	25	30	35	40
pH	3.1	4.2	4.8	5.2	5.6	6.0	11.2	11.6	12.1	12.4	12.5	12.6

What indicator would you use for this titration? Use the graph to explain your choice. (7)

(*c*) A student was given samples of the following salts:

sodium sulfate (Na₂SO₄)   **sodium sulfite (Na₂SO₃)**   **potassium sulfate (K₂SO₄)**

    (*i*)   What test could be carried out to distinguish between the sodium salts and the potassium salt? (4) What observation would you make in this test? (6)

    (*ii*)   Describe the test which could be carried out to distinguish between the sulfate salts and the sulfite salt. (15)

_____

11. Answer any **two** of the parts (*a*), (*b*) or (*c*) (2 × 25)

(*a*) State *Le Chatelier's principle*. (7)

A gaseous mixture of hydrogen, iodine and hydrogen iodide form an equilibrium according to the following equation.

$$H_{2(g)} + I_{2(g)} \rightleftharpoons 2HI_{(g)}$$

(*i*) Write an expression for the equilibrium constant, K_c, for this system. (6)

(*ii*) The value of the equilibrium constant, K_c, for this reaction is 50 at 721 K. If 2 moles of hydrogen iodide gas were introduced into a sealed vessel at this temperature calculate the amount of hydrogen iodide gas present when equilibrium is reached. (12)

(*b*) The diagram shows a sketch of the trend in the first ionisation energies for the elements 3 to 10 in the periodic table.

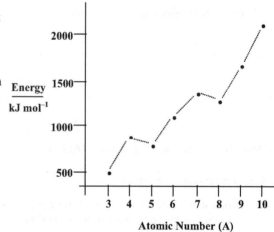

(*i*) Account for the general increase in ionisation energies across these elements. (7)

(*ii*) Explain why the ionisation energies of element number 4 and 7 are exceptionally high relative to the general trend. (12)

(*iii*) How does the definition of second ionisation energy differ from that of first ionisation energy? (6)

(*c*) Answer part **A** or part **B**

A

What is the chemical formula for ozone? State **one** beneficial effect of the ozone layer. (7)

CFCs are believed to be the main cause of damage to the ozone layer.

(*i*) What are CFCs? What use is made of CFCs? (6)

(*ii*) Explain how CFCs may give rise to ozone depletion. (12)

or

B

The structure of a buckminsterfullerene with 60 atoms is drawn on the right.

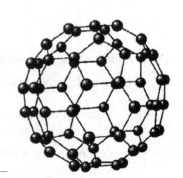

(*i*) Atoms of what element make buckminsterfullerenes? (4)

(*ii*) Name **two** other covalent macromolecular crystals formed by this element. What are the binding forces in each of these crystals? (15)

Give **one** use for **each** of these two substances. (6)

AN ROINN OIDEACHAIS AGUS EOLAÍOCHTA

LEAVING CERTIFICATE EXAMINATION, 2002

CHEMISTRY - HIGHER LEVEL

TUESDAY, 18 JUNE - AFTERNOON 2.00 to 5.00

400 MARKS

Answer **eight** questions in all

These **must** include at least **two** questions from **Section A**

All questions carry equal marks (50)

Information

Relative atomic masses: H = 1, C = 12, O = 16, Na = 23, Cl = 35.5

Molar volume at s.t.p. = 22.4 l

Avogadro constant = 6×10^{23} mol^{-1}

Universal gas constant, R = 8.3 J K^{-1} mol^{-1}

Section A

Answer at least two questions from this section [see page 1 for full instructions]

1. Vinegar is a solution of ethanoic acid (acetic acid). Some bottles of vinegar are labelled "*White Wine Vinegar*".

   (a) What compound in white wine is converted to ethanoic acid in vinegar?
   What type of chemical process converts this compound to ethanoic acid? (8)

   The concentration of ethanoic acid in vinegar was measured as follows:
   A 50 cm³ sample of vinegar was diluted to 500 cm³ using deionised water. The diluted solution was titrated against 25 cm³ portions of a standard 0.12 M sodium hydroxide solution, using a suitable indicator.

   (b) Describe the procedure for accurately measuring the 50 cm³ sample of vinegar and diluting it to 500 cm³. (12)

   (c) Name the piece of equipment that should be used to measure the ethanoic acid solution during the titration. State the procedure for washing and filling this piece of equipment in preparation for the titration. Name a suitable indicator for this titration. (15)

   The titration reaction is

$$CH_3COOH + NaOH \rightarrow CH_3COONa + H_2O$$

   After carrying out a number of accurate titrations of the diluted solution of ethanoic acid against the 25 cm³ portions of the standard 0.12 M sodium hydroxide solution, the mean titration figure was found to be 20.5 cm³.

   (d) Calculate the concentration of ethanoic acid in the diluted vinegar solution in moles per litre and hence calculate the concentration of ethanoic acid in the original sample of vinegar.
   Express this concentration in terms of % (w/v). (15)

   _____

2. Soap is produced by the hydrolysis of vegetable and animal fats.

   (a) What is the principal chemical difference between vegetable and animal fats? (5)

   A sample of soap was prepared in a school laboratory as follows:
   Approximately 3 g of lard (animal fat), 2 g of sodium hydroxide pellets (an excess), and 25 cm³ of ethanol were placed in a round-bottomed flask. A condenser was fitted to the flask and the mixture was refluxed gently for 20 minutes (Diagram 1).

   Following the reflux, the apparatus was allowed to cool slightly and the arrangement of the apparatus was changed so that the ethanol could be removed by distillation (Diagram 2).

   The residue from the distillation flask was then dissolved in a minimum of hot water and the solution decanted into 75 cm³ of brine. The soap was then isolated.

   (b) Apart from the lard, sodium hydroxide and ethanol, what else should be added to the reaction flask prior to the reflux?
   Why was the mixture refluxed?
   Why was the ethanol added? (15)

   (c) Why was it desirable to remove the ethanol after the reflux? (9)

   (d) Why was a <u>minimum</u> of hot water used to dissolve the residue from the distillation? What is brine? (9)

   (e) Describe how the soap could be isolated from the mixture of soap and brine. Give <u>one</u> precaution that helps to ensure that the soap is free of sodium hydroxide. (12)

   _____

Diagram 1

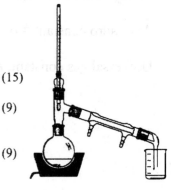

Diagram 2

3. To investigate the effect of concentration on a reaction rate, a student measured 100 cm³ of a 0.10 M solution of sodium thiosulfate into a conical flask, added 10 cm³ of 1.0 M hydrochloric acid, and then placed the flask on top of a cross on a sheet of white paper as shown in the diagram. The student noted the time (in minutes) taken for the cross to become obscured by the pale yellow precipitate formed in the solution. The reciprocal of the time (1/time) was used as a measure of the initial rate of the reaction.

Samples of the 0.10 M solution of sodium thiosulfate were diluted to make 100 cm³ portions of 0.08, 0.06, 0.04 and 0.02 M sodium thiosulfate. Each of these was, in turn, reacted with 10 cm³ of 1.0 M hydrochloric acid as described above. The results obtained are shown in the following table.

Concentration of sodium thiosulfate solution (M)	Time taken for the cross to become obscured (minutes)	1/time (min⁻¹) i.e. Rate
0.10	1.25	0.80
0.08	1.56	0.64
0.06	2.08	0.48
0.04	3.13	0.32
0.02	6.25	0.16

(a) Identify the pale yellow precipitate that obscured the cross on the sheet of paper. (5)

(b) Describe the procedure for preparing the 0.08 M solution of sodium thiosulfate from the 0.10 M solution. (12)

(c) Plot a graph to show the relationship between the initial rate of this reaction (1/time) and the concentration of the sodium thiosulfate solution. What conclusion can be drawn from the graph about the relationship between the rate of reaction and the concentration of the sodium thiosulfate? (18)

(d) Use the graph to determine how long it would have taken for the cross on the sheet of paper to become obscured if the student had used a 0.05 M sodium thiosulfate solution. (9)

(e) Explain why the reciprocal of the time (1/time) may be used as a measure of the initial rate of the reaction. (6)

_____

Section B

[See page 1 for instructions regarding the number of questions to be answered]

4. Answer **eight** of the following items (a), (b), (c), etc. (50)

    (a) What are *isotopes*?

    (b) Write the electronic configuration of a neutral copper atom.

    (c) Define *atomic orbital*.

    (d) The value of the dissociation constant for ethanoic acid is 1.8×10^{-5} l mol^{-1}. Calculate the pH of a 0.01 M solution of ethanoic acid.

    (e) What is the oxidation number of sulfur in $Na_2S_2O_3$?

    (f) How could you test for the presence of nitrate ions in aqueous solution?

    (g) What colour change will occur if concentrated sulfuric acid is added to the following equilibrium mixture? Give a reason for your answer.

$$2CrO_4^{2-} + 2H^+ \rightleftharpoons Cr_2O_7^{2-} + H_2O$$

    (h) What spectroscopic technique is used to detect heavy metals, e.g. lead, in environmental analysis?

    (i) State *Charles's law*.

    (j) Draw the structure and give the IUPAC name for CH_3CHO.

    (k) Answer **A** *or* **B**.

        A Write an equation for the photodissociation of ozone.

        B What are the structural differences between low-density and high-density poly(ethene)?

---

5. Refer to the data in the Mathematics Tables, pages 44 – 46, in answering this question.

    (a) Define *first ionisation energy*. (8)

    (b) Account fully for the trends in first ionisation energies of elements across the second period of the periodic table (i.e. Li to Ne). (15)

    (c) Account for the trend in first ionisation energies of the elements going down Group II of the periodic table, i.e. the alkaline-earth metals. (6)

The approximate values for the first eight ionisation energies of magnesium are given in the following table.

Ionisation	1st	2nd	3rd	4th	5th	6th	7th	8th
Ionisation energy (kJ mol^{-1})	730	1450	7750	10500	13600	18000	21500	25600

    (d) Explain why there is an increase in these ionisation energy values. (9)

    (e) Account for the dramatic increase in ionisation energy going from the second to the third ionisation. Between which two ionisations would you expect the next dramatic increase to occur if the data for further ionisation energies of magnesium were examined? Give a reason for your answer. (12)

---

6. Answer the questions (a) to (e) with reference to the compounds **A**, **B** and **C**.

$$C_3H_6 \qquad C_3H_7OH \qquad CH_3COCH_3$$
$$\textbf{A} \qquad\quad \textbf{B} \qquad\qquad \textbf{C}$$

(a) Which one of the three compounds would you expect to be the least soluble in water?
Give a reason for your answer. (8)

(b) Give the IUPAC names of compounds **A** and **C**. Name <u>both</u> isomers of compound **B**.
Name a compound that is a structural isomer of **C**. (15)

(c) Classify <u>each</u> of the compounds **A**, **B** and **C** as having one, two or three tetrahedrally bonded carbon atoms. (9)

(d) Compound **C** can be synthesised from compound **A** in two steps, with one of the isomers of **B** as the product of the first step. Name suitable reagents for each of the steps. (12)

(e) Compound **C** is a solvent. Give a common use for this solvent. (6)

---

7. Mass spectrometry and gas chromatography are widely used instrumental techniques in chemistry.

(a) Give <u>one</u> application of <u>each</u> of these techniques. (8)

(b) What are the main principles on which <u>each</u> of these techniques is based? (18)

(c) What are the fundamental processes that occur in a mass spectrometer? (15)

(d) HPLC is another chromatographic technique.
What do the letters HPLC stand for? State <u>one</u> application of this technique. (9)

---

8. The following hydrocarbons can all be used as fuels.

methane (CH_4)   **butane (C_4H_{10})**   **2,2,4-trimethylpentane (C_8H_{18})**

(a) Butane is a major component of LPG. What do the letters LPG stand for? (5)
Draw <u>two</u> structural isomers of butane. (6)

(b) Methane is a major component of natural gas.
Why are mercaptans often added to natural gas?
What environmental change or effect is associated with the release of methane to the atmosphere?
Apart from leaking gas pipes, name a major source from which methane is released to the atmosphere. (9)

(c) What structural feature of 2,2,4-trimethylpentane results in it having a high octane rating?
Give <u>one</u> other structural feature which increases the octane number of a hydrocarbon. (6)

(d) Define *heat of combustion* of a compound. (6)

(e) The combustion of butane is described by the following balanced equation.
$$2C_4H_{10(g)} + 13O_{2(g)} \longrightarrow 8CO_{2(g)} + 10H_2O_{(l)}$$

Calculate the heat of combustion of butane given that the heats of formation of butane, carbon dioxide and water are –125, –394 and –286 kJ mol^{-1}, respectively. (18)

---

9. (a) What property of water makes it very useful in the human body as a medium in which chemical reactions occur, and also allows it to become polluted or contaminated very easily in other situations? (5)

The treatment of a water supply for domestic use may involve several stages.

   (i) These stages may include *sedimentation, flocculation* and *filtration*.
   Describe what happens at each of these three stages. (18)

   (ii) Various chemicals are often added in other stages of water treatment.
   Identify one other stage in water treatment which involves the addition of a chemical to the water.
   Name one chemical added during this stage and state why this chemical is added. (9)

   (b) (i) Distinguish between the primary and secondary stages of sewage treatment. (12)

   (ii) What is the purpose of tertiary treatment? (6)

_____

10. Answer **two** of the parts (a), (b) and (c). (2×25)

   (a) Define *oxidation number*. (4)

   (i) Using oxidation numbers, identify which species is being oxidised and which species is being reduced in the following reaction. (12)

$$MnO_4^- + Cl^- + H^+ \rightarrow Mn^{2+} + Cl_2 + H_2O$$

   (ii) Hence, or otherwise, balance the equation. (9)

   (b) (i) What is the colour of the light associated with the line emission spectrum of sodium? (4)

   (ii) Explain how line emission spectra occur. (12)

   (iii) What evidence do line emission spectra provide for the existence of energy levels in atoms? (6)

   (iv) Why is it possible for line emission spectra to be used to distinguish between different elements? (3)

   (c) State *Le Chatelier's principle*. (7)

When 30 g of ethanoic acid and 23 g of ethanol were placed in a conical flask and a few drops of concentrated sulfuric acid added, an equilibrium was set up with the formation of ethylethanoate and water.
The equilibrium is represented by the following equation.

$$CH_3COOH + C_2H_5OH \rightleftharpoons CH_3COOC_2H_5 + H_2O$$

When the equilibrium mixture was analysed it was found to contain 10 g of ethanoic acid.

   (i) Write the equilibrium constant expression, K_c, for this reaction. (6)

   (ii) Calculate the value of the equilibrium constant, K_c. (12)

_____

11. Answer **two** of the parts (a), (b) and (c). (2×25)

(a) (i) In what type of household product would you expect to find sodium hypochlorite? (4)

(ii) A solution of sodium hypochlorite, NaOCl, is labelled as having a concentration of 5% (w/v). Express the concentration of the sodium hypochlorite solution in grams per litre. (6)

100 cm³ of this 5% (w/v) solution were reacted with excess chloride ion and acid according to the equation.

$$OCl^- \;+\; Cl^- \;+\; 2H^+ \;\rightarrow\; Cl_2 \;+\; H_2O$$

(iii) How many molecules of chlorine gas were liberated? (9)

(iv) What volume would this quantity of chlorine gas occupy at s.t.p.? (6)

(b) What are *alpha-particles* (α-particles)? (7)

Describe the experiment carried out by Rutherford and his co-workers that led to the discovery of the nucleus. Explain how Rutherford interpreted the results of this experiment to conclude that the atom has a nucleus. (18)

(c) Answer either part **A** *or* part **B**.

A

Distinguish between a batch and a continuous production process. (6)

Answer both of the following questions. (i) and (ii), in relation to <u>one</u> of the following processes:

ammonia manufacture   **nitric acid manufacture**   **magnesium oxide manufacture**

(i) In relation to your chosen chemical industry state <u>one</u> reason in favour of the Irish location of this industrial plant. (4)

(ii) Give a brief outline of the processes carried out in the manufacture of the main product, giving balanced chemical equations where relevant. (15)

or

B

Aluminium is extracted from bauxite.

(i) Where in Ireland is bauxite purified to produce alumina? (4)

(ii) Outline the steps involved in the extraction of alumina from bauxite, giving balanced chemical equations where relevant. (15)

(iii) Give <u>two</u> reasons why it is preferable to produce aluminium by recycling rather than by extracting it from its ore. (6)

AN ROINN OIDEACHAIS AGUS EOLAÍOCHTA

LEAVING CERTIFICATE EXAMINATION

CHEMISTRY - HIGHER LEVEL

REVISED SAMPLE PAPER, FEBRUARY 2002

---

3 HOURS DURATION

---

400 MARKS

Answer **eight** questions in all

These **must** include at least **two** questions from **Section A**

All questions carry equal marks (50)

Information

Relative atomic masses: H = 1, C = 12, N = 14, O = 16, Na = 23, Cl = 35.5, Cr = 52.

Molar volume at s.t.p. = 22.4 l

Avogadro constant = 6×10^{23} mol^{-1}

Universal gas constant, R = 8.3 J K^{-1} mol^{-1}

1 Faraday = 96 500 C

1. A student carried out an experiment in order to determine the concentration of sodium hypochlorite in a sample of household bleach. A 25.0 cm³ sample of the bleach was diluted to 250 cm³. A 25.0 cm³ portion of this diluted solution was added to an excess of acidified potassium iodide solution and titrated against a standard 0.21 M sodium thiosulfate solution. The average titration figure was 20.7 cm³.

The equations for the reactions are:

$$ClO^- + 2I^- + 2H^+ \rightarrow Cl^- + I_2 + H_2O$$

$$2S_2O_3^{2-} + I_2 \rightarrow S_4O_6^{2-} + 2I^-$$

(a) Explain why it was necessary to dilute the sample of bleach. (5)

(b) Briefly describe the procedure for accurately diluting the sample of bleach to 250 cm³. (12)

(c) The student added approximately 20 cm³ of dilute sulfuric acid and 10 cm³ of 0.5 M potassium iodide to the conical flask containing the diluted bleach.
What piece of apparatus is suitable to measure out these volumes of liquids? (3)

(d) Why was an <u>excess</u> of potassium iodide necessary?
What colour change was observed in the conical flask when the sulfuric acid and potassium iodide were added to the bleach? (6)

(e) Name the indicator used in this titration and describe how the end point was detected.
When was the indicator added during the titration? (12)

(f) Calculate the concentration of sodium hypochlorite in the household bleach in moles per litre.
Express this concentration in terms of % w/v. (12)

_____

2. (a) Reflux and distillation are both used in the laboratory preparation of ethanoic acid.

    (i) State the function of **each** of these procedures. (8)

    (ii) Draw a labelled diagram of the arrangement of apparatus for a reflux. (15)

(b) The diagram shows the apparatus used in the extraction of clove oil from cloves by steam distillation.

    (i) Explain why the clove oil could not be distilled directly from ground cloves. (12)

    (ii) Explain the function of the tube marked **X**. (6)

    (iii) What is collected at **Y**? Describe its appearance. (9)

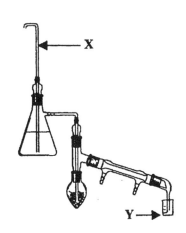

_____

3. A student carried out an experiment to measure the relative molecular mass of a volatile liquid.

   (a) Give **one** example of a liquid that would be suitable for use in this experiment. (5)

   (b) Draw a labeled diagram of an apparatus that could be used to determine the relative molecular mass of the liquid. (12)

   (c) In carrying out this experiment it is necessary to measure
       (i) the mass and
       (ii) the volume of vapour.
       Describe how **both** of these quantities are measured. (18)

   (d) Indicate **one** source of error in this experiment. (3)

   (e) In an experiment to find the relative molecular mass of a volatile liquid, a mass of 0.12 g of the liquid was vaporised by heating it at 100 $^\circ$C in a suitable apparatus. If the volume of the vapour was 84.5 cm^3 and the pressure was 9.5×10^4 Pa, calculate the relative molecular mass of the volatile liquid. (12)

Section B
[See page 1 for instructions regarding the number of questions to be answered]

4. Answer **eight** of the following parts (a), (b), (c) etc. (50)

   (a) Rutherford's experiment which led to the discovery of the nucleus involved bombarding particles at a thin foil. What was the nature of the bombarding particles and from what material was the foil made?

   (b) Nicotine, a colourless oil, is found in cigarettes. On analysis it is found to have an empirical formula of C_5H_7N. If the relative molecular mass of nicotine is 162, find its molecular formula.

   (c) Name the **two** reagents used to detect the presence of phosphate ions in solution.

   (d) Complete the following nuclear equation:

$$^{23}_{11}\text{Na} \longrightarrow \underline{\quad\quad} + {}^{0}_{-1}e$$

   (e) How many atoms are present in 2 moles of ammonia?

   (f) With what, in the petroleum industry, do you associate the following compound?

$$CH_3C(CH_3)_2CH_2CH(CH_3)_2$$

   (g) What is the difference between a *strong base* and a *weak base* according to the Arrhenius theory of acids and bases?

   (h) What is the effect of discharging untreated sewage into a lake on oxygen levels in the water? Explain your answer.

   (i) Write a balanced equation to describe the reaction that occurs at the anode when an electric current is passed through acidified water.

   (j) Define *radioactivity*.

   (k) Answer either **A** *or* **B**

     A Name **two** properties of CFCs that made them suitable for everyday uses.

     B Poly(tetrafluoroethene) is a useful polymer. Indicate the structure of the polymer, showing **two** repeating units.

---

5. (a) Refer to the data provided in the Mathematical Tables pages 44 – 46 in answering this question.

     Define *ionisation energy*. (8)

     Plot a graph of ionisation energy (y-axis) versus atomic number for the elements 11 to 18 inclusive. (15)

     Account fully for the trends in ionisation energies indicated by the graph. (15)

   (b) Mendeleev and Moseley are historically important figures in chemistry. Each contributed to the development of the periodic table of the elements.

     Briefly summarise the contributions of Mendeleev in this respect.

     What was Moseley's contribution to the development of the periodic table? (12)

---

6. Study the organic compounds A, B, C and D and answer the questions below:

C_2H_6	C_2H_4	CH_3CHO	CH_3OH
A	**B**	**C**	**D**

    (a) Which compound contains only one planar carbon in its molecules?   (5)

    (b) Name the compounds **A, B, C** and **D**.   (12)

    (c) Which **two** of these compounds can be easily converted to chloroethane?   (6)
        Outline the conditions and mechanism for **one** of these conversions.   (15)

    (d) Outline a possible synthetic route by which compound **B** could be converted to compound **C**.   (12)

---

7. (a) What piece of equipment is used for the accurate measurement of heats of combustion of substances?   (5)

       Define *heat of combustion* of a substance.   (6)

       Given that the standard heats of formation of water, carbon dioxide and ethyne are
       $-286, -394$ and 227 kJ mol^{-1}, respectively, calculate the heat of combustion of ethyne.   (12)

    (b) Draw a fully labelled energy profile diagram for the combustion of ethyne.   (12)

       List the bonds broken and the bonds formed in the combustion of ethyne.   (12)

       Give **one** major use of ethyne.   (3)

---

8. The following techniques all have applications in medicine, forensic science, pollution monitoring or in the chemical industry.

    mass spectrometry   **gas chromatography**   **high-performance liquid chromatography**
           infra-red spectrometry   **ultra-violet spectrometry**

In the case of **three** of these techniques outline

    (a) **one** application of **each** technique chosen, $(2 \times 5, 4)$

    (b) the principles on which **each** technique chosen is based. (3×12)

---

9. *Le Chatelier's principle* states that when a system at equilibrium is disturbed, the system responds so as to minimise the disturbance.

(a) In a chemical context, what do you understand by system at equilibrium? (8)

(b) What types of change could constitute a disturbance to a system at equilibrium? (12)

(c) Identify **one** simple chemical equilibrium reactions which can be set up in the school laboratory, which respond to one of the disturbances indicated in your answer part to (b) and which can be used to illustrate Le Chatelier's principle. (15)

(d) Two moles of hydrogen iodide placed in a sealed 2 litre vessel at 683 K decomposed to form hydrogen and iodine. The decomposition is represented by the equation

$$2HI \rightleftharpoons H_2 + I_2$$

If the value of the equilibrium constant, K_c, is 0.0156 at this temperature, find the number of moles of hydrogen iodide present at equilibrium. (15)

_____

10. Answer any **two** of the parts (a), (b) and (c). (2×25)

(a) Describe a laboratory preparation of ethanal.

(i) Give the name and structure of the organic compound chosen as the starting material. (7)

(ii) Identify the other reagents needed. (6)

(iii) Indicate the precautions which should be taken to maximise the yield of ethanal. (12)

(b) Define the *rate of a chemical* reaction. (7)

The rate of a chemical reaction may depend on a number of factors including
(i) the concentration of reactants (ii) particle size and (iii) temperature.

Describe simple laboratory experiments to illustrate the effect of **any two** of these factors on the rate of a chemical reaction. (18)

(c) Define *energy level*. (7)

In 1913 when Neils Bohr proposed his model for the structure of the atom he made a number of assumptions. The most important was that electrons in atoms occupied fixed energy levels or shells and could only absorb or release energy by moving from one energy level to another.

Outline the spectral evidence which exists to support this assumption for the hydrogen atom. (18)

_____

11. Answer any **two** of the parts (a), (b) and (c). (2×25)

(a) (i) Why is chlorine added to swimming-pool water? (4)

(ii) Explain the meaning of the term *free chlorine*. (6)

(iii) Chlorine is not normally added to swimming-pool water in the form of gaseous chlorine. Give the name <u>or</u> formula of a compound that is commonly used as a source of chlorine. (6)

(iv) Describe briefly the procedure used to estimate the concentration of free chlorine using either a comparator <u>or</u> a colorimeter. (9)

(b) A sample of ethanoic acid was prepared by reacting 8.5 cm^3 of ethanol (density 0.8 g cm^{-3}) with an acidified solution containing 38.56 g of sodium dichromate, $Na_2Cr_2O_7.2H_2O$.

The reaction may be represented by the equation

$$3C_2H_5OH + 2Cr_2O_7^{2-} + 16H^+ \rightarrow 4Cr^{3+} + 3CH_3COOH + 11H_2O$$

After purification, it was found that 4.3 g of ethanoic acid were formed.

(i) What is meant by *limiting reagent?* (4)

(ii) Determine the limiting reactant. (12)

(ii) Calculate the percentage yield of ethanoic acid. (9)

(c) Answer part **A** *or* part **B**

A (i) Sodium chloride is a crystalline material. What is meant by the term crystal? (7)

State the contribution of Dorothy Hodgkin to crystallography. (6)

(ii) Give **one** example of a molecular crystal and **one** example of a covalent macromolecular crystal. (6)

(iii) Compare the properties of molecular crystals and covalent macromolecular crystals under the headings: *binding forces*, *melting point* and *hardness*. (9)

or

B (i) Explain the meaning of the term *co-product* as used in industrial chemistry. (4)

With regard to an industrial case study undertaken by you, answer the following questions.

(ii) What was the feedstock used? (6)

(iii) Indicate how the feedstock was prepared from the raw materials. (9)

(iv) Outline the waste disposal and effluent control carried out. (6)

LEAVING CERTIFICATE EXAMINATION

CHEMISTRY – HIGHER LEVEL

SAMPLE PAPER 1

3 HOURS DURATION

400 MARKS

Answer **eight** questions in all
These **must** include at least two questions from Section A
All questions carry equal marks (50)

Information

Relative Atomic Masses: H = 1, C = 12, N = 14, O = 16, Na = 23, Mg = 24, S = 32, Cl = 35.5, K = 39, Ca = 40, Cr = 52, Fe = 56, Cu = 63.5, I = 127.

Molar volume at s.t.p. = 22.4L

Avogadro constant = 6×10^{23} mol^{-1}

Universal gas constant, R = 8.3 J K^{-1} mol^{-1}

Section A (100 marks)

Answer at least two questions from this section [see first page of this paper for full instructions]

1. (a) Describe what you would observe if a large piece of zinc was placed in a dilute solution of copper (II) sulfate and left for 24 hours. Write an equation for the reaction. What is this type of reaction usually called? (15)

    (b) Briefly describe the steps you would take to check if a solution contained nitrate ions and explain what you would see if the result was positive. (20)

    (c) When doing a flame test what substance is used to moisten the crystals being tested? What colours are produced by Li and by Cu? (9)

    (d) What type of spectrum is produced in a flame test? (6)

---

2. A group of students was asked to analyse an iron tablet to determine the amount of iron sulfate it contained and compare this with the value stated on the packet. They weighed five tablets and then crushed them using a pestle and mortar. The crushed tablets were transferred to a beaker containing 100 cm³ of dilute sulfuric acid and dissolved fully. The solution was then transferred to a 250 cm³ volumetric flask and made up to the mark using deionised water. The flask was inverted several times and then a pipette was used to transfer 25 cm³ of the solution to a conical flask. This was then titrated using a standard solution of potassium permanganate.

    (i) Why did the students take five tablets? (3)

    (ii) Why are the iron tablets crushed when trying to dissolve them? (3)

    (iii) Give two precautions taken when transferring the crushed tablets to the volumetric flask. (6)

    (iv) The volumetric flask is inverted several times before a sample is taken from it. What feature of the flask makes this necessary and why is it done? (6)

    (v) Describe how the burette is prepared for the titration. (9)

    (vi) In potassium permanganate titrations an acid is usually added to the conical flask. What acid is usually added and why is it added? What would you see if it was not added? (12)

    (vii) When reading the level of potassium permanganate solution in a burette, which point do you take the reading from? (3)

    (viii) How is the end-point of the titration identified? (3)

    (ix) The students' answer was markedly different from that shown on the packet. Assuming the value given on the packet is correct, suggest a possible source of error in the students' experiment. (5)

---

3. (a) Draw a labelled diagram of the apparatus you would use to produce and collect ethyne in the laboratory. (18)

    (b) Phosphine gas often occurs as an impurity in ethyne. How would you remove the phosphine from the ethyne? (6)

    (c) Ethyne is often described as an *unsaturated hydrocarbon*. Explain the two words in italics. (6)

(d)   How would you show that ethyne is unsaturated? Name a reagent you would use to
      show that ethyne is unsaturated and describe what you would observe when this   (9)
      reagent is applied to a sample of ethyne gas and shaken.

(e)   Describe what you would see if ethyne is burned in air.   (6)

(f)   Give a wide-scale use of ethyne.   (5)

Section B (300 marks)

[See first page of this paper for instructions regarding the number of questions to be answered]

4.   Answer **eight** of the following parts (a), (b), (c), etc. All parts carry the same number of (10×5)
     marks.

(a)   How many (i) protons and (ii) neutrons are present in the ion $_{11}^{23}Na^+$?

(b)   What type of bonding occurs between (i) hydrogen and oxygen in a molecule of
      water and (ii) molecules of water in a crystal of ice?

(c)   Give the systematic (IUPAC) name for $CH_3CH_2CH_2CH_3$.

(d)   Give two common uses of radioisotopes.

(e)   Calculate the relative atomic mass of the element X whose composition was
      found to be 70% $_{29}^{63}X$ and 30% $_{29}^{65}X$.

(f)   What is a strong acid according to the Brønsted-Lowry Theory? Name one.

(g)   Calculate the volume occupied by 8 g of oxygen at 20 $^{\circ}$C and 200 kPa.

(h)   What happens in secondary treatment of sewage?

(i)   Write the electronic configuration (s,p, etc.) of (i) a sulfur atom and
      (ii) the chloride ion.

(j)   What would you see happening when chlorine gas is bubbled through a solution
      of sodium bromide? What does this tell you about chlorine and bromine?

(k)   State the shape of the following two molecules (i) CO_2 and (ii)NH_3.

(l)   Why does HF have a higher boiling point than HCl?

(m)   What is meant by the term *half-life* of an element?

(n)   Calculate the pH of 0.2 M NaOH.

---

5.   (a)   Petrol is obtained from crude oil in an oil refinery. Name the process used to obtain
            the petrol from the crude oil.   (6)

     (b)   Give the name and structural formula of the substance found in petrol which is
            assigned an octane number of 100?   (6)

     (c)   What is meant by octane number?   (5)

     (d)   What lead compound used to be added to petrol? Explain why it was added to the
            petrol and give a reason why it is no longer added to petrol.   (9)

     (e)   Name two features of the structure of alkanes which would make them less prone to
            knocking.   (6)

     (f)   Oxygenates are often added to petrol. Give an example of an oxygenate and explain (9)
            why it is added to the petrol.

     (g)   Explain the term *catalytic cracking* and briefly say why it is used.   (9)

---

6. The following data was recorded by a pupil studying the rate of a certain chemical reaction. The pupil reacted 2 cm strips of magnesium ribbon with dilute nitric acid at various temperatures.

Temperature [^{o}C]	70	60	50	40	30	20	10
Time for magnesium strip to disappear (s)	2.5	6.0	10.0	20.0	40.0	80.0	160
Rate [1000/s]	400	167	100	50	25	12	6.25

   (i)   Write an equation for the reaction between magnesium and nitric acid. (6)
   (ii) At what point would you record the time for each reaction? (6)
   (iii) Use the data given above to draw a graph of rate against temperature. (12)
   (iv) What is the approximate relationship between temperature and rate? (8)
   (v)   Give two reasons why the rate is faster at 35 ^{o}C than at 20 ^{o}C. (9)
   (vi) Which value for rate do you think is most likely to be incorrect?
         Give a reason for your choice. (6)
   (vii) Give a danger associated with the gas produced. (3)

   _____

7. (a) Draw diagrams to represent the structure of (i) benzene and (ii) methylbenzene. (6)

   (b) Methylbenzene is often used in the laboratory in preference to benzene.
        Give a reason for this. (3)

   (c) Benzene and methylbenzene are described as aromatic compounds.
        What does aromatic mean? (3)

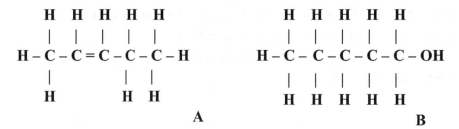

   (d) Name the above compounds **A** and **B**. (6)

   (e) Compound (B) can undergo an elimination reaction.
        Write an equation for this reaction. Name the reagents involved and give another
        name for this type of reaction. (12)

   (f) Outline the mechanism for the reaction between bromine and ethene. (15)

   (g) Is benzene soluble in water? Give a reason for your answer. (5)

   _____

70

8. (a) Define (i) heat of combustion and (ii) heat of formation of a compound. (12)

$$2H_2S_{(g)} + SO_{2(g)} = 3S_{(S)} + 2H_2O_{(l)}$$

(b) Using the information given below

$H_{2(g)} + S_{(s)} = H_2S_{(g)}$ $\quad$ $\Delta H = -21$ kJ mol^{-1}

$S_{(s)} + O_{2(g)} = SO_{2(g)}$ $\quad$ $\Delta H = -297$ kJ mol^{-1}

$H_2 + \frac{1}{2}O_{2(g)} = H_2O_{(l)}$ $\quad$ $\Delta H = -286$ kJ mol^{-1}

Calculate the heat of reaction for the above reaction. (15)

Whose law did you use when solving the above problem? (3)

(c) What would the effect of raising the temperature be on the yield of sulfur? Give a brief explanation of your answer. (8)

(d) Draw an energy profile diagram of an exothermic reaction and superimpose on it the profile one might expect if a catalyst were used. (12)

---

9. (a) Briefly describe the contribution of each of the following to the development of atomic theory: (a) Rutherford, (b) Chadwick and (c) Bohr. (18)

(b) What are the vertical columns in the Periodic Table called? What do the elements in each column have in common? (6)

(c) Linus Pauling coined the term *electronegativity*. What does electronegativity mean, and how does it change as one goes (i) across a row and (ii) down a column of the Periodic Table?

Give a reason for your answer to either (i) or (ii). (21)

(d) What forces hold the particles together in (i) a piece of ice and (ii) a crystal of iodine? (5)

---

10. Answer any **two** of the parts (a), (b) and (c).

(a) Explain the term *eutrophication*. (4)

What do the letters BOD stand for and what is this a measure of? (4)

When doing the Winkler Test for oxygen content of water, what is the significance of a white precipitate when Winkler's Reagent is added to the water? (4)

In the event of a white precipitate forming, a fresh sample should be taken. What should be done to this sample before the test is administered again? (4)

4 cm^3 of 0.1 molar sodium thiosulfate solution was needed to reach the end point of the titration of 200 cm^3 of water sample. What is the dissolved oxygen content of the sample of water? (9)

(b) Give an example of each of the following types of bonding.

   (i) Polar covalent (5)

   (ii) Dative (5)

   (iii) Hydrogen (5)

   (iv) Ionic (5)

How do you know that the example you have given in (i) is polar covalent and not ionic? (5)

(c) $CaCO_{3(s)} + 2HCl_{(aq)} = CaCl_{2(aq)} + CO_{2(g)} + H_2O_{(l)}$

In the above reaction, 5 g of $CaCO_3$ was reacted with 150 cm³ of 1M HCl.

What mass of $CaCl_2$ would be formed? (9)

What volume of CO_2 [measured at s.t.p.] would be produced? (6)

Name the limiting chemical. (5)

How would you test for the presence of the chloride ion in a solution? (5)

_____

11. Answer any **two** of the parts (a), (b) and (c).

(a)   State Le Chatelier's Principle (4)

$$PCl_{3(g)} + Cl_{2(g)} \rightleftharpoons PCl_{5(g)}$$

Write the K_c expression for the above reaction. (6)

Given the following equilibrium concentrations:

$PCl_3 = 0.025$ mol/L ; $Cl_2 = 0.1$ mol L ; $PCl_5 = 0.1$ mol/L

Calculate K_c for the reaction. (6)

In each of the following cases state what the effect on the yield of PCl_5 would be.
In one case explain your answer briefly:
(i) Adding more $Cl_{2(g)}$ (ii) Increasing the pressure on the system. (9)

(b)   Define pH. (4)

Ammonia solution is a weak base. Explain the term weak base according to the Brønsted-Lowry Theory. (3)

Calculate the pH of a 0.1 M solution of ammonia given that $K_b = 1.8 \times 10^{-5}$. (12)

What would be a suitable acid to use when calculating the concentration of ammonia by titration and which indicator would you use in the titration? (6)

(c)   Answer part **A** or **B**.

   A   Answer the following with regard to an industrial case study you have undertaken.
   (i) Explain two of the terms: feedstock, co-products or batch process. (6)
   (ii) Give two reasons for the factory being placed in its present location. (4)
   (iii) Give an example of a fixed cost and a variable cost. (6)
   (iv) Mention a method of waste disposal or effluent control in effect in the factory. (3)
   (v) Name two examples of important chemicals produced in Ireland other than the one in your case study. (6)

   B   (i) Draw a labelled diagram of the apparatus used to extract sodium on an industrial scale. (14)
   (ii) Give the equation for the reaction that takes place at each electrode. (8)
   (iii) Give a large scale use of sodium. (3)

LEAVING CERTIFICATE EXAMINATION

CHEMISTRY – HIGHER LEVEL

SAMPLE PAPER 2

3 HOURS DURATION

400 MARKS

Answer **eight** questions in all
These **must** include at least two questions from Section A
All questions carry equal marks (50)

Information

Relative Atomic Masses: H = 1, C = 12, N = 14, O = 16, Na = 23, Mg = 24, S = 32, Cl = 35.5, K = 39, Ca = 40, Cr = 52, Fe = 56, Cu = 63.5, I = 127.

Molar volume at s.t.p. = 22.4L

Avogadro constant = 6×10^{23} mol^{-1}

Universal gas constant, R = 8.3 J K^{-1} mol^{-1}

Section A (100 marks)

Answer at least two questions from this section [see first page of this paper for full instructions]

1. Ethanoic acid can be prepared in the laboratory by reacting ethanol with excess acidified potassium dichromate solution.

   (i) Draw a labelled diagram of the apparatus you would use to prepare the ethanoic acid in this way. Explain (a) why the apparatus is arranged in this way and (b) why the mixture is heated for around 30 minutes. (18)

   (ii) State and explain the colour change you would expect to see as the reaction proceeds. (9)

   (iii) State how you would rearrange the apparatus to collect the ethanoic acid. (3)

   (iv) The ethanoic acid would contain impurities. Name two possible impurities and explain briefly how you would remove them. (12)

   (v) Small particles of glass beads or pumice stone are added to the reagents in the flask before it is heated. What are they called and why are they added? (8)

   _____

2. In using a standard solution of 0.1 M sodium thiosulfate to calculate the concentration of an iodine solution, a 20 cm^3 pipette was used to place the iodine solution into the conical flask. The average titration figure was 15.0 cm^3 of sodium thiosulfate solution.
   The equation for the reaction is: $I_2 + 2\ S_2O_3^{2-} \rightarrow S_4O_6^{2-} + 2I^-$

   (i) What indicator would you use in this experiment? State when you would add it and explain why you would add it at this time. What colour change would you observe? (15)

   (ii) When doing the titration, some of the solution in the conical flask got splashed high up the side of the conical flask. What should you do to rectify this situation? Why does this not affect the result of the experiment? (6)

   (iii) Describe in detail how you would prepare the burette for the titration. (12)

   (iv) Calculate the concentration of the iodine solution in mol/L. (9)

   (v) What is a primary standard and why is iodine not suitable as a primary standard? (8)

   _____

3. Explain the term *redox reaction.* (5)

   (a) (i) Chlorine water is added to some sodium bromide solution in a test tube. Describe what you would see happening and write a half equation for the reaction taking place. Give a use for this reaction. (15)

   (ii) Chlorine water is added to a solution of sodium sulfite in a test tube. What happens to the sulfite ion? How can you show that this has happened? [State the reagents used and any changes observed.] (15)

   (b) (i) Write an equation for the reaction which takes place when magnesium ribbon is added to a solution of copper(II) sulfate.

   (ii) Describe what you would see happening as the reaction proceeds.

   (iii) Name the substance oxidised and the substance reduced.

   (iv) What is the name [other than redox] given to this type of reaction?

   (v) What information does it give about copper and magnesium? (15)

   _____

Section B (300 marks)

[See first page of this paper for instructions regarding the number of questions to be answered]

4. Answer **eight** of the following parts (a), (b), (c), etc. All parts carry the same number of marks. (10 × 5)

   (a)   Describe how you would test for the presence of phosphate ions $[PO_4^{3-}]$ in aqueous solution.

   (b)   Name the two ions removed in tertiary treatment of sewage.

   (c)   Identify the species (i) $1s^2 2s^2 2p^6 3s^2 3p^3$ and (ii) $[1s^2 2s^2 2p^6 3s^2 3p^6]^{2+}$.

   (d)   Give an example of an autocatalyst and name the reactants involved.

   (e)   What is the conjugate acid of NH_3?

   (f)   Name and give the formula of a compound that causes temporary hardness in water.

   (g)   Calculate the pH of a 0.1 M solution of CH_3COOH given that $K_a = 1.7 \times 10^{-5}$.

   (h)   How many atoms are there in 250 cm³ of methane at STP?

   (i)   What instrument is used to measure heats of reaction accurately?

   (j)   What gas is produced at the anode during the electrolysis of sodium sulfate solution using inert electrodes?

   (k)   How many grams of NaOH would be required to make 250 cm³ of 0.1 molar solution?

   (l)   Draw the structural formula for 3,3 dichloroprop-1-ene.

   (m)   What mass of copper would be needed to produce 2.56 g of copper(II) oxide?

   (n)   EDTA solution is used to determine the hardness of water samples. Name the indicator used in these titrations and state the colour change.

   _____

5. Refer to the data provided in the mathematical tables pages 44–46 in answering this question.

Atomic Number	5	6	7	8	9	10
1st Ionisation Energy	799	1090	1400	1310	1680	2010

   (a)   Above is a table showing the variation in First Ionisation Energy with Atomic Number. Draw a graph using this data. (9)

   What is meant by First Ionisation Energy of an element? (6)

   Give a reason for the general increase in First Ionisation Energy as atomic number increases. (3)

   Explain why the increase is interrupted at one point. (6)

   (b)   What is an atomic orbital? (3)

   Draw a diagram of a set of p orbitals. (6)

   How are the electrons arranged in the 3s and 3p sublevels of the element of atomic number 16? (6)

   (c)   Explain the following terms: (i) atomic number, (ii) relative atomic mass and (iii) isotopes. (11)

   _____

6.

A $-C\overset{\displaystyle O}{\underset{\displaystyle OH}{\Big\langle}}$

B $R-C\overset{\displaystyle O}{\underset{\displaystyle R'}{\Big\langle}}$

C $-C\overset{\displaystyle O}{\underset{\displaystyle H}{\Big\langle}}$

D $R-C\overset{\displaystyle O}{\underset{\displaystyle O-R'}{\Big\langle}}$

(a) What is meant by the term *functional group*? (6)

(b) In each of the above cases state the homologous series to which the functional group belongs and give the name of the first member of the series. (20)

(c) Short-chain alcohols are soluble in water while long-chain alcohols are not. How do you account for this difference? (9)

(d) Using your knowledge of organic chemistry, give an example of an elimination reaction. (6)

(e) Write an equation to show what happens when sodium metal is dropped into ethanol. Name the organic product. (9)

———————————

7.

$$H_{2(g)} + I_{2(g)} \rightleftharpoons 2\,HI_{(g)}$$

(a) Write the equilibrium constant expression (K_c) for the above reaction. (6)

(b) What is meant by the term *chemical equilibrium?* (5)

(c) 2.54 g of iodine was mixed with 1.0 g of hydrogen in a closed vessel at 773 K. K_c for the reaction at this temperature is 49.
Calculate the equilibrium masses of each substance in the reaction vessel. (21)

(d) Why is it not necessary to know the volume of the reaction vessel in this case? (6)

(e) Would (i) increasing the pressure on the reaction vessel or (ii) introducing a catalyst change the position of equilibrium? Explain your answer in each case. (12)

———————————

8. (a) Use electron dot diagrams to show how the following atoms bond. In each case state the type of bond involved.
(i) magnesium and oxygen (7)
(ii) oxygen and hydrogen (6)
The triple bond between nitrogen atoms in a molecule of nitrogen gas consists of two types of bonds. What are these two types of bonds? In each case specify the orbitals involved. (12)

(b) Draw a simple diagram of a mass spectrometer and explain what three of the parts do. (25)

———————————

9. (a) State the types of chromatography most suited to the following tasks:
(i) To determine blood alcohol levels.
(ii) To test for the presence of growth promoters in meat.
(iii) To separate the components of food dyes. (9)

(b) Give three ways that the octane rating of a fuel may be increased and in each case state by what means the octane rating is improved. (18)

Fossil fuels are a non-renewable resource and they will eventually run out. Hydrogen is predicted by many as the fuel of the future.

Give two ways of making hydrogen on a large scale and write an equation to illustrate one of the reactions you have mentioned. (12)

Mention one major advantage and one major disadvantage of hydrogen as a fuel. (6)

(c)   The heats of combustion and kilogram calorific value of methane and hydrogen are given below. Explain why the kilogram calorific value of hydrogen is much greater than methane even though the heat of combustion of hydrogen is much lower.   (5)

	Heat of Combustion kJ mol^{-1}	Kilogram Calorific Value kJ kg^{-1}
Methane	-890	55625
Hydrogen	-286	143000

10. Answer any **two** of the parts (a), (b) and (c).
(a)   Explain why increasing the temperature of the reactants increases the rate of a reaction.   (6)

Give two other factors that affect the rate of chemical reactions.   (6)

Give an example of a heterogeneous catalyst and write the equation for the reaction it catalyses.   (9)

What are biological catalysts normally called? Name one.   (4)

(b)   On analysis, a compound was found to contain 40% C, 6.7% H and 53.3 % O. Its relative molecular mass was 60.

Calculate its empirical formula and then its molecular formula.   (9)

To which homologous series does it belong?   (3)

Draw a diagram to show its structural formula.   (3)

Write an equation for its reaction with methanol and name the organic product of the reaction.   (10)

(c)

Name the apparatus shown which can be used to electrolyse acidified water.   (4)

What substance are the electrodes made of? Why is this substance used?   (6)

What gas is produced at the anode?   (3)

If 20 cm^3 of this gas was produced, what volume of gas would be produced at the other electrode?   (3)

Write an equation for the reaction that takes place at the anode.   (6)

How would you identify the gas produced at either electrode?   (3)

11. Answer any **two** of the parts (a), (b) and (c).

(a) A student took 2000 cm³ of water from a bucket and filtered it through a previously weighed dry filter paper. The paper was dried and then re-weighed. 500 cm³ of water from the bucket was then placed in a weighed dry beaker and evaporated to dryness. The results obtained by the student are recorded below.

Mass of dry filter paper at start = 12.75 g
Mass of filter paper after filtering and drying = 12.86 g

Mass of beaker at start = 132.55 g
Mass of beaker after evaporation = 132.84 g

Using the above data, what results would the student have got for:
(i) suspended solids;
(ii) dissolved solids. (12)

The student made a basic error in the method employed. State the error and explain (6) what the student should have done to get the correct answer.

What substance is added to water in the purification treatment to remove (7) suspended solids and what is the name given to the process it triggers?

(b) Radon-226 loses an alpha particle when it undergoes radioactive decay and (6) carbon-14 loses a beta particle.
What is (i) an alpha particle and (ii) a beta particle?

Write equations to show what happens to each atom as it decays. (13)

Explain the term *half-life.* (3)

Give a use of the carbon-14 isotope. (3)

(c) Answer part **A** or **B.**

A (i) Name two gases that cause acid rain. Give a major source of each (12) of these gases.

(ii) Write an equation to show how one of these gases forms acid rain. (5)

(iii) Give three major effects of acid rain and explain how one of these (8) can be minimised.

B (i) Name three addition polymers and give a use for each. (9)

(ii) Select one of the polymers you have mentioned above and show how (6) it forms.

(iii) List the five stages in the recycling of plastics. (10)

LEAVING CERTIFICATE EXAMINATION

CHEMISTRY – HIGHER LEVEL

SAMPLE PAPER 3

3 HOURS DURATION

400 MARKS

Answer **eight** questions in all
These **must** include at least two questions from Section A
All questions carry equal marks (50)

Information

Relative Atomic Masses: H = 1, C = 12, N = 14, O = 16, Na = 23, Mg = 24, S = 32, Cl = 35.5, K = 39, Ca = 40, Cr = 52, Fe = 56, Cu = 63.5, I = 127.

Molar volume at s.t.p. = 22.4L

Avogadro constant = 6×10^{23} mol^{-1}

Universal gas constant, R = 8.3 J K^{-1} mol^{-1}

Section A (100 marks)

Answer at least two questions from this section [see first page of this paper for full instructions]

1. A group of students was asked to calculate the percentage of water of crystallisation in a sample of sodium carbonate. They weighed out accurately 5.20 g of hydrated sodium carbonate crystals on a clock glass and dissolved these in water. They transferred this solution, with washings to a 250 cm³ volumetric flask and made it up to the mark using deionised water. Using a pipette, they put 25 cm³ of this sodium carbonate solution into a conical flask and added a few drops of indicator. They then added their standard solution of 0.1 M HCl from the burette until the indicator changed colour. They did a total of three titrations and their results were as follows:

    21.1 cm³; 20.6 cm³; 20.7 cm³

    The equation for the reaction is: $Na_2CO_3 + 2HCl = 2NaCl + CO_2 + H_2O$

    (i)   Which indicator would you use for this titration? Give a reason for your choice of indicator? State the colour change seen at the end point. (12)

    (ii) Describe what should be done to the pipette before it is used to transfer the sodium carbonate to the conical flask, and how you would ensure that exactly 25 cm³ was transferred. (9)

    (iii) What value should be used for the titration figure? (3)

    (iv) Using the information given above calculate: (i) the molarity of the sodium carbonate solution, (ii) the number of moles in the 250 cm³ volumetric flask and (iii) the mass of sodium carbonate. (18)

    (v)   Calculate the mass of water in the original crystals and hence find the percentage of water of crystallisation in the crystals. (8)

    _____

2. A student set up the following apparatus to measure the rate of decomposition of hydrogen peroxide solution. The total volume of gas collected every minute is shown in the table below.

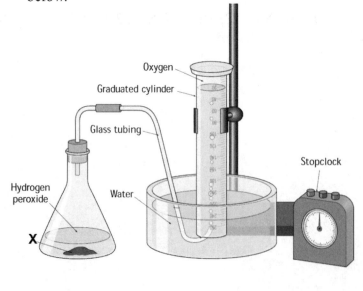

Time	Volume
0	0
1	25
2	40
3	47.5
4	51.3
5	53.2
6	55
7	56
8	56.5
9	57
10	57
11	57

    (i)   Name the substance X in the diagram and say what it is acting as in the reaction. (6)

    (ii) How would you start the reaction at the appointed time? (3)

    (iii) Write an equation for the reaction that occurs. (6)

(iv)   Draw a graph using the data given and calculate the instantaneous rate at 2 minutes and at 5 minutes. (15)

(v)   Account for the change in rate between the two times. (6)

(vi)   Would the amount of substance X alter (i) the rate at which the gas was produced and (ii) the total amount of gas produced? (6)

(vii)   Mention a safety precaution you should take during the experiment and suggest a precaution you could take to make the results more accurate. (8)

---

3.   (a)   Draw a labelled diagram of the apparatus you would use to extract clove oil from whole cloves. (18)

(b)   Why are cloves harvested just before the flower opens? (3)

(c)   Give two uses of clove oil. (6)

(d)   What is the purpose of the steam trap and why are the cloves not simply heated directly? (6)

(e)   Suggest a reason why it is recommended that gloves be worn during this experiment. (3)

(f)   The clove oil is collected as an *emulsion.* Explain the term emulsion and state one method of extracting the clove oil from the emulsion. What is the process of removing the oil from cloves called? (12)

(g)   Name another substance extracted by the same method. (2)

Section B (300 marks)
[See first page of this paper for instructions regarding the number of questions to be answered]

4.   Answer **eight** of the following parts (a), (b), (c), etc. All parts carry the same number of marks. (10×5)

(a)   Name the colour that would be produced in fireworks by salts containing the following metals: (i) copper and (ii) potassium.

(b)   Give the oxidation number of chromium in $Cr_2O_7^{2-}$.

(c)   Write the electron configuration[s,p] of a magnesium ion.

(d)   Define electrolysis.

(e)   Write down the Equation of State for an ideal gas.

(f)   What mass of NaOH would be required to make 500 cm^3 of 5% (w/v) solution?

(g)   State the shape of the following: (i) NH_3 and (ii) $AlCl_3$.

(h)   Draw the structural formula of methylbenzene.

(i)   In which stage of sewage treatment does biological oxidation take place?

(j)   Name the separation technique in which a solvent moves along an absorbent material such as paper or alumina.

(k)   Give (i) the conjugate acid and (ii) the conjugate base of HCO_3^-.

(l)   An element contains the following isotopes in the stated abundances:

68% $^{68}_{29}Cu$ and 32% $^{65}_{29}Cu$. Calculate its relative molecular mass correct to two decimal places.

(m)   In the electrolysis of water using Hoffmann's voltameter, 0.02 g of hydrogen was produced at the negative electrode. What volume of oxygen [measured at s.t.p.] would have been produced at the anode?

(n)   How many atoms of hydrogen are there in 560 cm^3 of hydrogen gas at s.t.p.?

---

5. (a) 100 cm^3 of 1 M HCl was placed in a polystyrene cup and the temperature recorded. At the same time, 100 cm^3 of 2 M NaOH was placed in another polystyrene cup and its temperature was also measured. The contents of the two cups were mixed and the resulting temperature was recorded and was observed to increase by $6.5\,^{\circ}\text{C}$. Assuming the specific heat capacity and density of the mixture is that of water [$4.2 \text{ kJ kg}^{-1} \text{ K}^{-1}$ and 1 g cm^{-3} respectively]:

Why were polystyrene cups used instead of glass beakers? (6)

How would you ensure that the temperature is recorded accurately? (6)

Calculate the heat of reaction. (15)

What other name can be given to this heat of reaction? (3)

(b) $CH_4 = C + 4 H \quad \Delta H = +1648 \text{ kJ mol}^{-1}$

Calculate the value of the C – H bond in methane. (4)

Do all C – H bonds have the same value? Explain your answer. (6)

(c) *Dehydrocyclisation* and *isomerisation* are used to improve the octane rating of fuels. Explain these terms. (10)

---

6. Ethanol reacts with ethanoic acid according to the following equation:

$$CH_3CH_2OH + CH_3COOH \rightleftharpoons CH_3CH_2COOC_2H_5 + H_2O$$

3 g of ethanoic acid was reacted with 2.3 g of ethanol and allowed to come to equilibrium at 293 K. When the reaction was stopped it was found that 1.0 g of ethanoic acid was left at equilibrium.

(i) Name the organic product of the reaction and state the homologous series to which it belongs. (6)

(ii) Write the equilibrium constant expression K_c and calculate the equilibrium constant for the reaction. (21)

(iii) How would you determine the amount of ethanoic acid left experimentally? Name two reagents you would need to use to do this. (9)

(iv) Calculate the % yield of the reaction and say if this is a reasonable value. (14)

---

7. (a) Draw a labelled diagram to show how ethene can be prepared and collected using ethanol in the laboratory. (9)

(b) What would you see happening if ethene was reacted with bromine water? What does this tell you about the structure of ethene? (6)

(c) Show in detail the mechanism by which bromine reacts with methane and give an example of the evidence there is to back up this mechanism. (24)

(d) Ethylbenzene is an aromatic hydrocarbon. Draw the structure of ethylbenzene and explain the term *aromatic hydrocarbon*. (11)

---

8. (a) Describe how you would identify phosphate ions [PO_4^{3-}] in solution. (9)

Calculate the volume occupied by 17.25 g of chlorine gas at $20\,^{\circ}\text{C}$ and 400 kPa. (8)

On analysis, a hydrocarbon was found to contain 92.3 % C and 7.7 % H. Its relative molecular mass is about 80. (12)
What is its molecular formula and structural formula?

(b)	Give the shapes of the following molecules: (i) NH_3, (ii) CO_2 and (iii) HCHO.	(9)

(c)	Define reduction and explain how reduction is involved in the purification of copper.	(12)

9.	(a)	What is meant by the term *transition elements*?	(6)

Transition elements have three characteristic properties. State two of these.	(6)

Explain the term *first ionisation energy*.	(5)

Why is the first ionisation energy of titanium higher than that of scandium?	(9)

Why is the second ionisation energy of titanium greater than the first?	(9)

What type of spectra are produced by the excited atoms of an element?	(3)

To what use did Niels Bohr put these spectra?	(3)

(b)	Show the arrangement of electrons in the 2p orbitals of nitrogen.	(3)

Draw the shape of these orbitals.	(3)

Nitrogen has greater stability than oxygen. Give a reason for this.	(3)

10.	Answer any **two** of the parts (a), (b) and (c).

(a)	Electrolysis is used in the purification of copper. Draw a labelled diagram of the apparatus used to do this and specify which is the pure and which is the impure copper.	(10)

Write equations for the reactions that take place at each electrode.	(6)

What happens to the impurities in the copper?	(3)

What is electroplating? Name a metal that is commonly electroplated and state which electrode the object to be electroplated is connected to.	(6)

(b)	There are two main mechanisms of catalysis. Name these two mechanisms and give an example of one of them, stating the catalyst and the reactants involved.	(9)

Catalytic converters are fitted to modern motor cars. Name one of the main elements used as the catalyst and briefly describe its function.	(9)

Explain the term heterogeneous catalyst. Give an example.	(7)

(c)	What is an acid according to the Brønsted-Lowry Theory?	(4)

In the following equation, identify the acids and bases and a conjugate acid base pair.	(9)

$$NH_3 + H_2O \rightarrow NH_4^+ + OH^-$$

Give a reason for the following: (i) toothpaste is slightly basic, (ii) sodium bicarbonate is put on bee stings, (iii) dock leaves are rubbed on nettle stings and (iv) farmers often spread lime on land.	(12)

11.	Answer any **two** of the parts (a), (b) and (c).

(a)	Explain the term *eutrophication* and name two of the main types of compounds that cause it?	(12)

How does sewage treatment help prevent eutrophication occurring?	(7)

Heavy metals can also cause serious pollution. Give an example of such a metal and a likely source of this pollution. What is a common method of removing these metals from water?	(6)

(b)   Describe what you would expect to see if a test tube of ethyne is burned in air.   (6)

Ethyne is an unsaturated compound. Describe how you could demonstrate this in the lab.   (6)

Write an equation for the combustion of methane in excess air. Where are you most likely to encounter methane in your everyday life?   (9)

What are mercaptans used for?   (4)

(c)   Answer either part **A** or **B**.

    A   Using information gathered in your industrial case study, answer the following questions:

        (i)   Why was the site chosen?   (3)

        (ii)   What type of process (batch or continuous) is used in the production process? Give one advantage of this process.   (6)

        (iii)   What are the sources of the raw materials?   (6)

        (iv)   What has to be done to the raw materials before they can be used?   (6)

        (v)   Name a co-product and what is done with it at the end of the process.   (4)

    B   (i)   Name a common ore of iron.   (3)

        (ii)   Give the equation for the reduction of the ore to iron.   (5)

        (iii)   Give an equation for the production of slag.   (5)

        (iv)   What is the iron leaving the blast furnace called?   (3)

        (v)   In making steel the iron is purified and then alloyed with a non-metal. Name this non-metal.   (3)

        (vi)   Name a metal that can be added to the steel to change its properties and say what this type of steel is called or how its properties are changed.   (6)

LEAVING CERTIFICATE EXAMINATION

CHEMISTRY – HIGHER LEVEL

SAMPLE PAPER 4

3 HOURS DURATION

400 MARKS

Answer **eight** questions in all
These **must** include at least two questions from Section A
All questions carry equal marks (50)

Information

Relative Atomic Masses: H = 1, C = 12, N = 14, O = 16, Na = 23, Mg = 24, S = 32, Cl = 35.5, K = 39, Ca = 40, Cr = 52, Fe = 56, Cu = 63.5, I = 127.

Molar volume at s.t.p. = 22.4L

Avogadro constant = 6×10^{23} mol^{-1}

Universal gas constant, R = 8.3 J K^{-1} mol^{-1}

Section A (100 marks)

Answer at least two questions from this section [see first page of this paper for full instructions]

1. (a) Draw a labelled diagram of the apparatus you would use to make and collect ethanal in the laboratory. (9)

   (b) Small porcelain chips were added to the contents of the flask before heating. Give a reason for adding these chips. (3)

   (c) Why is it normal to stop heating the acid before adding the alcohol/dichromate mixture from the funnel? (6)

   (d) Explain why it is advisable to remove the ethanal as quickly as possible from the reaction vessel. (4)

   (e) State the method you would use to collect the ethanal and give a reason for using this method (6)

   (f) Name one of the main impurities in the ethanal and describe how you would remove it. (6)

   (g) Describe the colour change you would see during the reaction and explain why this colour change occurs. (9)

   (h) Ethanal is soluble in water. Name and draw the feature of the ethanal molecule that is responsible for its solubility in water. (7)

---

2. A bucket of water was collected from a stream and brought back to the lab to check its BOD. Two bottles were filled with water from the bucket. One of the samples was placed in a dark cupboard and the other had its oxygen content measured immediately. When measuring the oxygen content, small amounts of two concentrated liquids were added and a brown precipitate was formed. Concentrated sulfuric acid was added until the brown precipitate dissolved. 100 cm³ samples of the solution were place in a conical flask and titrated using a sodium thiosulfate solution from a burette with a suitable indicator. It took 8 cm³ of 0.025 M thiosulfate to react completely with each 100 cm³ sample. Some days later the other sample was tested and it was found that its oxygen content was 3.4 p.p.m.

   (i) What should have been done to the bottles before the water samples were collected? Give a reason for doing this. (6)

   (ii) Why was the second bottle put in the cupboard, and how long should it have been left there? Give a reason for using a dark cupboard. (9)

   (iii) Suggest a reason for the liquids added being concentrated. (3)

   (iv) Occasionally a white precipitate is formed in a water sample instead of a brown one. What would the formation of this white precipitate tell you? (3)

   (v) Name the indicator used and state the colour change observed. The indicator should be added at a certain point: state this point and explain why it is not added earlier. (12)

   (vi) Calculate the oxygen content of the sample in p.p.m. (12)

   (vii) What was the B.O.D. of the water? (5)

---

3. In a titration to find the concentration of ethanoic acid in vinegar, a sample of vinegar was diluted by pipetting a 25 cm³ sample into a 250 cm³ volumetric flask. This was then made up to the mark with deionised water and mixed well. The vinegar solution was then added to the burette using a funnel. The funnel was removed before the titration was carried out. 20 cm³ of 0.1 M sodium hydroxide solution was pipetted into a conical flask and a few drops of indicator were added. The vinegar was added from the burette and the following results were recorded:

10.5 cm³ ; 10.2 cm³ ; 10.2 cm³

The equation for the reaction is:

$$CH_3COOH + NaOH \rightarrow CH_3COONa + H_2O$$

   (i) By what factor was the vinegar diluted? (3)
  (ii) What is meant by the term **standard solution**? (3)
 (iii) Why was the filter funnel removed before the titration was begun? (3)
 (iv) What indicator would you use, and what colour change would you observe at the end of the titration. Why would you only add a few drops of indicator? (12)
  (v) List the precautions you should take when preparing and using the pipette? (9)
 (vi) Calculate the concentration of the ethanoic acid in the vinegar. (12)
 (vii) Draw the structure of the functional group of the ethanoic acid in vinegar. (3)
(viii) Ethanoic acid is a weak acid. What does this mean? (5)

Section B (300 marks)

[See first page of this paper for instructions regarding the number of questions to be answered]

4. Answer **eight** of the following parts (a), (b), (c), etc. All parts carry the same number of marks. (10×5)

  (a) How many (i) neutrons and (ii) electrons are there in the ion $_{26}^{56}Fe^{3+}$?

  (b) Distinguish between **isotopes** and **isomers.**

  (c) Why do alcohols have higher boiling points than the corresponding alkanes?

  (d) What volume would be occupied by 1.5×10^{22} molecules of hydrogen at STP?

  (e) Write an equation to represent the anode reaction in the purification of copper.

  (f) Give an example of an autocatalyst and the reaction it catalyses.

  (g) The following two scientists: (i) Chadwick and (ii) Thompson made major contributions to the development of chemistry. What were their contributions?

  (h) What is made by the Contact Process and what catalyst is used in this process?

  (i) What mass of $KMnO_4$ would be needed to make 200 cm³ of 2% (w/v) solution?

  (j) Draw the structural formula of the monomer used to make polyethene.

  (k) Give the name and structural formula of the aromatic compound with molecular formula C_7H_8.

  (l) Draw the structural formula of 2-chloropent-2-ene.

  (m) Name the scum formed when soap reacts with hard water.

  (n) Calculate the pH of a 0.2 M solution of the weak acid ethanoic acid given that the acid dissociation constant for ethanoic acid $(K_a) = 1.7 \times 10^{-5}$.

---

5. (a) Each of these homolegous series has a C3 homolog (a member containing three carbon atoms). Draw the structural formula and name the C3 homolog for each of the following:
  (i)   a secondary alcohol
  (ii) an aldehyde
  (iii) a carboxylic acid
  (iv) alkene   (16)

(b) Write the equation by which ethanol is produced naturally from sugars. Name this process and give the name and source of the enzyme involved.
Explain the term enzyme.   (12)

Give two uses of ethanol other than its use in drink.   (6)

Why is it particularly dangerous to drink methanol or drinks that contain it, e.g. methylated spirits?   (4)

(c) Briefly describe the mechanism of the reaction between bromine and ethene.   (12)

---

6. (a) Explain what is meant by heat of combustion, and name an apparatus used to measure it accurately.   (6)

Give an example of an endothermic reaction [equation not required] and say how this information is displayed when writing an equation.   (6)

(b) Write the equation for the heat of formation of ethane.   (5)

Given the following information:

$$C_{(s)} + O_{2(g)} = CO_{2(g)} \qquad\qquad \Delta H = -393 \text{ kJ mol}^{-1}.$$

$$H_{2(g)} + \tfrac{1}{2} O_{2(g)} = H_2O_{(g)} \qquad \Delta H = -286 \text{ kJ mol}^{-1}.$$

$$2\,C_2H_6 + 7\,O_{2(g)} = 4\,CO_2 + 6\,H_2O_{(g)} \qquad \Delta H = -3120 \text{ kJ mol}^{-1}.$$

Calculate the heat of formation of ethane.   (12)

(c) Explain the term auto-ignition and how it is related to octane number.   (6)

Name and draw the structural formula of the compound that is assigned an octane number of 100.   (6)

In each case state which of the following hydrocarbon pairs would have the higher octane rating: (9)
  (i)   Long chain – short chain
  (ii) Branched chain – unbranched chain
  (iii) Straight chain – cyclic

---

7. Refer to the data provided in the mathematical tables pages 44–46 in answering this question.

(a) Name the scientist who discovered sodium and state the process he used in doing so.   (9)

(b) In each of the following cases name an element which:
  (i)   is a liquid at room temperature;
  (ii) sublimes;
  (iii) is the most reactive metal;
  (iv) is radioactive;
  (v)   imparts a lilac colour to a bunsen flame.   (15)

(c)　Explain why the atomic radius of magnesium is less than that of
(i) sodium and (ii) calcium. (6)

(d)　What type of bond is formed between atoms of hydrogen and sulfur? Give a reason
for your answer. What is the formula of the compound formed when these two
elements react, and what is the shape of the molecule? (12)

(e)　What was the contribution of the following scientists to the development of the
Periodic Table: (i) Dobereiner (ii) Newlands? (8)

---

8. (a)

$$N_{2(g)} + 3 H_{2(g)} \rightleftharpoons 2 NH_{3(g)} \qquad \Delta H = -50 \text{ kJ mol}^{-1}$$

What is the name given to the process represented by the above equation? (4)

Give three conditions normally associated with the process. (9)

State Le Chatelier's Principle. (6)

What would be the effect of raising the temperature of the reaction mixture?
Explain your answer. (9)

(b)　Ethanol and benzoic acid react according to the equation:

$$C_2H_5OH + C_6H_5COOH = C_6H_5COO\ C_2H_5 + H_2O$$

The equilibrium constant for this reaction at $100\ ^\circ$C is 2.73. Calculate the
concentration of all species at equilibrium if 138 g of ethanol is reacted with
1 mole of benzoic acid in a 1 L flask. (18)

Why is it important to state the temperature when giving an equilibrium constant? (4)

9.　In an experiment to investigate rates of reaction, a group of students reacted 3.0 g of zinc
foil with an excess of 1.0 M hydrochloric acid and measured the volume of gas collected
at regular intervals. Their results are listed below.

Time (s)	0	15	30	45	60	75	90	105	120	135	150	165
Volume (cm³)	0	24	36	45	51	55	58	60	61	62	62	62

(i)　Draw a labelled diagram of the apparatus you would use to do this experiment. (8)

(ii)　Write a balanced equation for the reaction of zinc with hydrochloric acid and
calculate the maximum volume of hydrogen [at s.t.p.] that could have been
produced by the reaction using the amount of zinc stated. (9)

(iii)　Give a possible reason for the difference between the calculated volume of gas and
the actual volume obtained. (3)

(iv)　Draw a graph of volume of gas produced against time. (12)

　　　Using the graph calculate:
　　　(a) the instantaneous rate at 80 seconds;
　　　(b) the time taken to produce 0.002 moles of hydrogen [measured at s.t.p.];
　　　(c) the number of moles of hydrogen produced after 1 minute. (18)

10.　Answer any **two** of the parts (a), (b) and (c).

(a)　Who discovered radioactivity? (4)

　　　Name the three types of particles produced by radioactive decay and say how
　　　penetrative each type is. (12)

　　　Give three uses of radioisotopes. (9)

(b)   Define electrolysis. (4)

Write the equations for the reactions which take place at the electrodes during the electrolysis of copper (II) sulfate using copper electrodes. (12)

What type of reaction takes place at the anode? Give a reason for your answer. (6)

What is this reaction used for? (3)

(c)   A sample of ethanal [CH_3CHO] was prepared by reacting 11.55 cm^3 of ethanol [C_2H_5OH] with 14.9 g of sodium dichromate $Na_2Cr_2O_7.2H_2O$.

Density of ethanol = 0.8 g cm^{-3}. It was found that 1.6 g of ethanal were formed.

$$3C_2H_5OH + Cr_2O_7^{2-} + 8H^+ = 3CH_3CHO + 2Cr^{3+} + 7H_2O$$

From the information given above, show which of the two reactants is the *limiting reactant* in this reaction. (10)

Calculate the percentage yield of ethanal. (15)

---

11.   Answer any **two** of the parts (a), (b) and (c).

(a)   Name three parts of a mass spectrometer and briefly describe the function of each part. (12)

Give two uses of the mass spectrometer. (6)

A sample of boron was analysed in a mass spectrometer and found to contain 81.4 % of $^{11}_{5}$B and 18.6% of $^{10}_{5}$B. Calculate the relative molecular mass of boron. (7)

(b)   What is meant by the term *temporary hardness*? (4)

Name or give the formula of two substances that cause it. (6)

When doing a titration to find out the hardness of a water sample, edta and Eriochrome Black T are used along with another substance. What is the name of the other substance and what is its function? (6)

5 cm^3 of a 0.01 M solution of edta are needed to react fully with 50 cm^3 of a sample of hard water. After boiling a sample of the same water it takes 3 cm^3 of a 0.01 M solution of edta to react with 50 cm^3 of the water sample. Calculate the values for the temporary and the permanent hardness of the water sample. (9)

(c)   Answer part **A** or **B**.

A   (i) Briefly describe the Greenhouse Effect and how it works. (9)
       (ii) Name a Greenhouse Gas other than CO_2. (4)
       (iii) Mention two possible results of global warming. (6)
       (iv) State two ways in which CO_2 can be removed from the atmosphere. (6)

B   (i) Describe two methods of protecting iron from rusting. (7)
       (ii) What is anodising? (6)
       (iii) Draw a labelled diagram of a voltaic cell using zinc and copper. (6)
       (iv) Would the same voltage be produced using zinc and lead? Explain your answer. (6)

LEAVING CERTIFICATE EXAMINATION

CHEMISTRY – HIGHER LEVEL

Information

Relative atomic masses: H = 1, C = 12, O = 16, Ca = 40.

Molar volume at s.t.p. = 22.4L

Avogadro constant = 6×10^{23} mol^{-1}

Universal gas constant, R = 8.3 J K^{-1} mol^{-1}

1 Faraday = 96 500 C

Additional Questions – May 2001

The following are examples of the type of questions appropriate to Section A on the examination paper.

Sample Question

Vinegar is an approximately 1 M solution of ethanoic acid (acetic acid, CH_3COOH).
You are required to accurately determine the concentration of a sample of vinegar diluted to one tenth of its original concentration. You are supplied with anhydrous sodium carbonate as a primary standard and all other common laboratory reagents.

(i) Starting with sodium carbonate (a primary standard), state what titrations you would carry out in order to determine the concentration of the diluted vinegar.
State the approximate concentration of each solution mentioned in your series of titrations.
What indicator is suitable for each titration involved? Give a reason for each choice of indicator. (36)

(ii) Describe how you would prepare 500 cm^3 of a solution of sodium carbonate of suitable concentration. (14)

Sample Question

Describe the laboratory preparation of ethanal. Your answer should include the following details:

(i) the organic compound chosen as the starting material and the other reagents and materials needed (12)

(ii) a labelled diagram of the assembly of apparatus and also the reaction conditions and (15)

(iii) details of how the product is isolated. (6)

Describe two simple diagnostic tests carried out on the product stating the reagents required, how the tests are carried out and any observations made during the tests. (17)

Sample Question

The tables show some data for two compounds which were purified in a school laboratory.

Compound	m.p. before purification / °C	m.p. after purification / °C
Benzoic acid	114 - 118	120 - 121

Compound	b.p. before purification / °C	b.p. after purification / °C
Ethanoic acid	110 - 113	120 - 121

(a) Give details of how the benzoic acid may have been purified. Illustrate your answer with appropriate diagrams.
State the evidence from the table to suggest that the compound has been purified. (30)

(b) Describe how the ethanoic acid may have been purified.
Illustrate your answer with an appropriate diagram. (15)
Ethanoic acid is corrosive. Draw or describe the hazard warning symbol which should be displayed on a container of ethanoic acid. (5)

Sample Question

The diagram shows an apparatus used to prepare ethanal from ethanol, using acidified sodium dichromate solution. The same reagents, but a different arrangement of apparatus is used to prepare ethanoic acid from ethanol.
The reactions involved are redox (oxidation-reduction) reactions, and the same colour change is observed in both reactions.

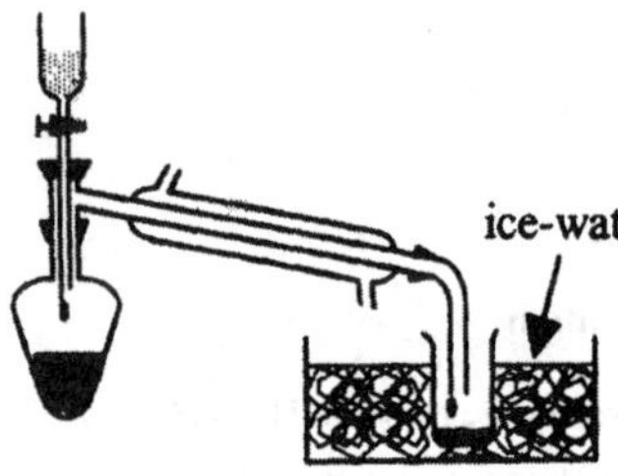

(i)   Why are anti-bumping granules placed in the flask? (4)

(ii) When carrying out the experiment, the students were instructed to remove the source of heat before adding the ethanol /sodium dichromate mixture. Explain the reason for this. (7)

(iii) Describe and account for the colour change involved in the reactions. (9)

(iv) Why is the receiving flask of ethanal surrounded by ice-water? (6)

(v)   In the preparation of ethanal, what two steps are taken to ensure that ethanal rather than ethanoic acid is produced? (9)

(vi) Apart from a colour change, what else is observed in the flask as the ethanol/sodium dichromate mixture is added to the hot, dilute sulfuric acid? (6)

(vii) What change in (a) the arrangement of apparatus and (b) the reaction conditions would be required to produce ethanoic acid? (9)

The following are examples of the type of questions appropriate to Section B on the examination paper.

Sample Question

(a) In 1913 when Neils Bohr proposed his model for the structure of the atom he made a number of assumptions. The most important was that electrons in atoms occupied fixed energy levels or shells and only absorb or release energy when moving from one energy level to another.
Outline the spectral evidence which exists to support this assumption for the hydrogen atom. (18)

(b) It quickly became obvious that the Bohr model had serious limitations and had to be revised. What were the limitations? (18)

(c) State two differences between the way Bohr described the atom in his 1913 model and our present understanding of the structure of the atom. (14)

Sample Question

(a) Write a brief note on the contribution of (i) John Dalton (ii) William Crookes and (iii) James Chadwick to the development of atomic theory. (20)

(b) Outline briefly the experiment performed by Rutherford and his co-workers that led to the discovery of the nucleus. Explain how Rutherford interpreted the results of this experiment. (12)

(c) In Mendeleev's Periodic Table the elements were arranged in order of increasing atomic weight (relative atomic mass). In the modern Periodic Table the elements are arranged in order of increasing atomic number. Explain the meaning of the underlined terms. (9)

(d) What would be the relative positions of argon and potassium in the Periodic Table if the elements were arranged in order of increasing relative atomic mass? (3)

(e) What is the electronic configuration of (i) a cobalt atom (ii) a magnesium ion (Mg^{2+})? (6)

2008. M33

Coimisiún na Scrúduithe Stáit
State Examinations Commission

LEAVING CERTIFICATE EXAMINATION, 2008

CHEMISTRY – ORDINARY LEVEL

THURSDAY, 5 JUNE – AFTERNOON 2.00 TO 5.00

400 MARKS

Answer **eight** questions in all

These **must** include at least **two** questions from **Section A**

All questions carry equal marks (50)

Information

Relative atomic masses: H = 1, O = 16, Mg = 24, S = 32, Cl = 35.5

Molar volume at s.t.p. = 22.4 litres

Avogadro constant = $6 \times 10^{23} \ \text{mol}^{-1}$

Section A

Answer at least <u>two</u> questions from this section [see page 1 for full instructions].

1. A group of students prepared a sample of ethanoic (acetic) acid, CH_3COOH, in the school laboratory as follows.

   A solution of ethanol, C_2H_5OH, in water was added in small portions to an aqueous solution of sodium dichromate(VI), $Na_2Cr_2O_7$, and sulfuric acid, H_2SO_4, contained in a flask immersed in ice-water (Diagram 1).

   When all of the ethanol solution had been added, the reaction mixture was refluxed for about thirty minutes (Diagram 2).

   At the end of the reflux period, the apparatus was rearranged and the ethanoic acid was removed from the reaction mixture by distillation (Diagram 3). The ethanoic acid was collected as a fraction which distilled between 115 °C and 118 °C.

   (a) Make a rough sketch of any one of these arrangements of apparatus in your answer-book and clearly indicate the direction in which the water should flow through the condenser. (8)

   (b) Explain why small pieces of glass or pumice stone were added to the reaction flask at the start of the experiment. (6)

   (c) What was the colour of the solution of sodium dichromate(VI) and sulfuric acid in the reaction flask before any of the solution of ethanol and water was added from the dropping funnel? (6)

   (d) Why was the solution of ethanol and water added in small portions? (6)

   (e) What colour was produced as the ethanol reacted with the sodium dichromate(VI)? (6)

   (f) Why was it important to reflux the reaction mixture? (6)

   (g) Why was a water bath not suitable for heating the flask during the distillation? (6)

   (h) A dilute solution (5-6 % w/v) of ethanoic acid (acetic acid) is used in food preservation and as a flavouring agent.
   What is the common name of this solution? (6)

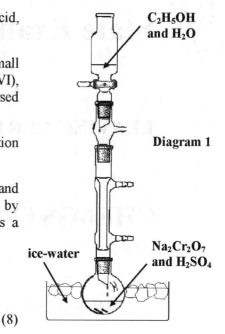

C_2H_5OH and H_2O

Diagram 1

ice-water

$Na_2Cr_2O_7$ and H_2SO_4

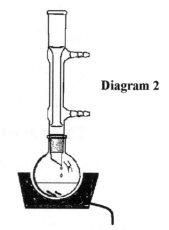

Diagram 2

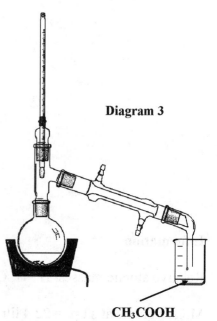

Diagram 3

CH_3COOH

2. A standard (0.05 M) solution of sodium carbonate, Na_2CO_3, was made up in the flask shown in the diagram. After making up the solution, it was used to find the concentration of a hydrochloric acid, **HCl**, solution.

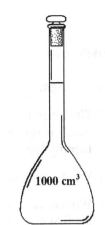

1000 cm³

(a) What term is used to describe the type of flask shown in the diagram? (5)

(b) What is a *standard solution*? (6)

(c) Outline the steps involved in making up the standard solution of sodium carbonate. (12)

(d) In the titrations carried out to find the concentration of the hydrochloric acid solution, what piece of equipment is usually used to measure the volume of

   (i) the sodium carbonate solution,

   (ii) the hydrochloric acid solution? (12)

(e) Name an indicator suitable for a titration involving sodium carbonate and hydrochloric acid solutions. State the colour of the mixture at the end point. (6)

(f) It was found that 25.0 cm³ of the 0.05 M sodium carbonate solution required 20.0 cm³ of the hydrochloric acid solution for exact neutralisation. The balanced equation for the titration reaction is:

$$Na_2CO_3 \ + \ 2HCl \qquad \rightarrow \qquad 2NaCl \ + \ H_2O \ + \ CO_2$$

Calculate the molarity of the hydrochloric acid, **HCl**, solution. (9)

---

3. Flame tests can be used to identify the metallic element present in a salt.

> Potassium nitrate (KNO_3)
>
> Sodium chloride ($NaCl$)
>
> Copper(II) chloride ($CuCl_2$)

(a) Copy the table below into your answer book and complete it, matching the correct salt from the list on the right with the colour it imparts to a Bunsen flame. (14)

FLAME COLOUR	Orange-yellow	Lilac	Green
SALT			

(b) Describe how you could carry out a flame test using one of these salts. (18)

(c) Where, outside the laboratory, would you be likely to see lights containing sodium vapour? (6)

(d) Some fireworks produce red light in the sky.
Name a metal whose salts are used in the manufacture of fireworks that produce red light. (6)

(e) What test could you carry out to confirm the presence of chloride ions in aqueous solution? (6)

Section B

[See page 1 for instructions regarding the number of questions to be answered.]

4. Answer **eight** of the following items (*a*), (*b*), (*c*), etc. (50)

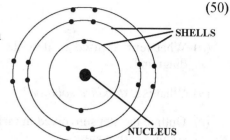

(*a*) The diagram on the right shows the arrangement of electrons in main energy levels (shells) for an atom of a particular element. Identify the element.

(*b*) What is an *endothermic reaction*?

(*c*) What is the trend in the size of atomic radii going down the first group of the periodic table?

(*d*) Name the piece of equipment used to measure the calorific values of foods and fuels.

(*e*) What is meant by the *octane number* of a fuel?

(*f*) Name the English scientist pictured on the right who identified, in the 1890s, electrons as negatively charged subatomic particles.

(*g*) Define *oxidation* in terms of electron transfer.

(*h*) Write the equilibrium constant (K_c) expression for the equilibrium:

$$2SO_2 \ + \ O_2 \ \rightleftharpoons \ 2SO_3$$

(*i*) Calculate the percentage by mass of magnesium in magnesium sulfate ($MgSO_4$).

(*j*) Identify **one** natural product that is extracted from plant material by steam distillation.

(*k*) Answer part **A** *or* part **B**.

    A   State **two** ways in which safety can be promoted at a chemical plant.

or

    B   Give any **two** characteristic properties of metals.

---

5. (*a*) Atoms are made up of protons, neutrons and electrons.

    (*i*) Copy the following table into your answer book and fill in the missing information. (17)

	Relative mass	Relative charge	Location
Proton	1		
Neutron			nucleus
Electron	1/1836	− 1	

    (*ii*) What information about subatomic particles is given by the atomic number of an element? (6)

(*b*) (*i*) Define *electronegativity*. (6)

    (*ii*) How are electronegativity values used to predict the type of bonding present in a compound? (6)

(*c*) The diagram on the right shows the bonding in a fluorine molecule, F_2. Dots (•) and crosses (×) represent the electrons.

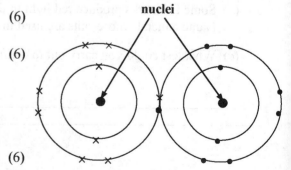

    (*i*) What type of chemical bond is found between the fluorine atoms in a fluorine molecule? (6)

    (*ii*) Name another type of chemical bond formed by fluorine. Give an example of a compound in which fluorine forms this type of bond. (9)

---

6. Hydrogen gas and the hydrocarbons ethyne and butane are all used as fuels.

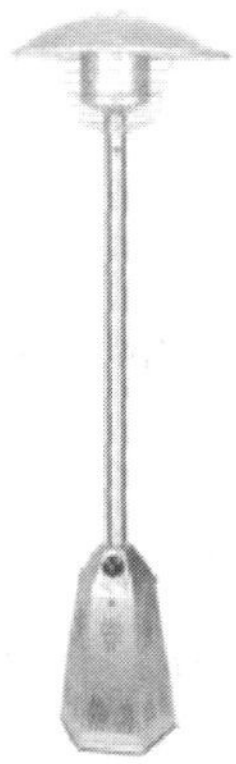

(a) What are (i) *hydrocarbons*, (ii) *fuels*? (8)

(b) (i) Which of the three fuels, named above, is a major component of liquid petroleum gas (LPG) used as a fuel in patio heaters?

(ii) Which of the three fuels is used as a fuel for space rockets?

(iii) Which of the three fuels has the common name acetylene and is used in high temperature cutting equipment? (15)

(c) Write structural formulas for the hydrocarbons ethyne and butane. (12)

(d) The diagram on the right shows a fractionating column used in oil refining. Crude oil is separated into fractions that come off through the outlet pipes on the right-hand side of the column.

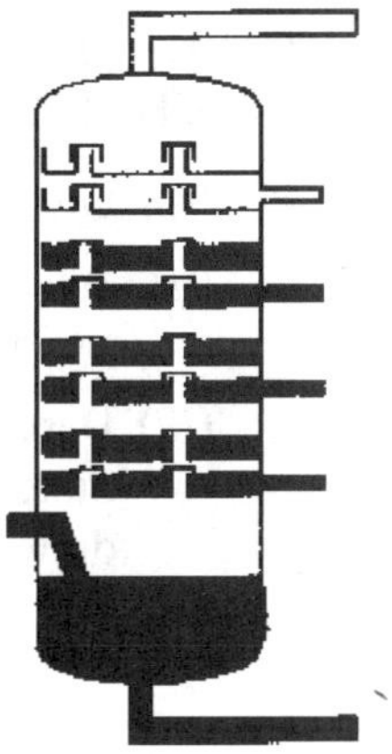

Name **one** of the fractions obtained by the fractionating process.
State whether this fraction is collected from high up, from the middle or from low down the fractioning column.
State **one** major use of this fraction. (15)

crude oil in

---

7. (a) In 1884, the Swedish chemist, Arrhenius, pictured on the right, proposed a new theory of acids and bases.

(i) How did Arrhenius define an acid? (5)

(ii) Give **one** example of a commonly used base and state **one** use made of it. (12)

(b) (i) Define pH. (6)

(ii) Describe how you could measure the pH of a solution. (9)

The concentration of a solution of hydrochloric acid, **HCl**, is 3.65 grams per litre.

(iii) What is the concentration of the solution in moles per litre? (9)

(iv) Calculate the pH of the solution. (9)

---

8. (a) The treatment of water for domestic use may involve each of the following stages.

sedimentation   **flocculation**   **filtration**   **chlorination**

fluoridation   **pH adjustment**

State the purpose of **four** of these stages <u>and</u> describe how the water is treated in each of the four stages you have chosen. (24)

(b) The treatment of domestic and industrial effluent is normally divided into three stages: **primary**, **secondary** and **tertiary**.

Explain what happens in each of these stages. (18)

(c) Give **two** environmental consequences of discharging untreated sewage into a river. (8)

---

9. Answer the questions below with reference to compounds **X**, **Y** and **Z** in the following reaction scheme.

$$CH_2CH_2 \longleftarrow CH_3CH_2OH \longrightarrow CH_3CHO$$
$$\textbf{X} \qquad\qquad \textbf{Y} \qquad\qquad \textbf{Z}$$

(a) Which **one** of the compounds **X**, **Y** or **Z** has <u>only</u> planar bonded carbon atoms? (5)

(b) Give the names of the compounds **X**, **Y** and **Z**. (9)

(c) Which of the three compounds **X**, **Y** or **Z**

(i) is found in concentrations of about 40-55% (v/v) in whiskey,

(ii) is used to make the plastic poly(ethene) [polythene]? (12)

(d) An apparatus suitable for the conversion of **Y** to **X** in a school laboratory is drawn on the right.

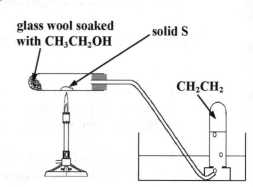

(i) Give the name or formula of the white solid **S**.

(ii) Why should the delivery tube be removed from the trough of water when the heating is stopped?

(iii) Describe one test you carried out on **CH₂CH₂**. State the observation you made and the conclusion drawn. (24)

---

10. Answer any **two** of the parts (a), (b) and (c). (2 × 25)

(a) The table shows data obtained when a hydrogen peroxide solution decomposed to form water and oxygen in the presence of a catalyst.

Time seconds	0	10	20	30	40	50	60	70
Volume of oxygen gas produced cm³	0	30	53	69	79	85	88	88

(i) On graph paper, plot the volume of oxygen produced (y-axis) against time (x-axis) (12)

(ii) Find from the graph the volume of oxygen produced in the first 15 seconds. (6)

(iii) Use the graph to find the time at which the reaction was finished. (7)

(b) Mass spectrometry (MS), gas chromatography (GC), high-performance liquid chromatography (HPLC) and thin-layer chromatography (TLC) are all used in analytical chemistry.

(i) In the case of **each** one of these analytical techniques state **one** important application of the technique. (16)

(ii) Choose one of these analytical techniques and explain the principle upon which it is based. (9)

(c) In the Haber process, nitrogen and hydrogen react to produce ammonia (**NH₃**).

$$N_{2\,(g)} + 3H_{2\,(g)} \rightleftharpoons 2NH_{3\,(g)} \qquad \Delta H = -92.4 \text{ kJ}$$

Le Châtelier's principle is applied in deciding the conditions required to give the best yield of the product.

(i) State *Le Châtelier's principle*. (7)

(ii) What does the symbol $\rightleftharpoons$ tell us about the reaction? (6)

Henri Le Châtelier

(iii) Using Le Châtelier's principle, state whether you would use high or low temperature, <u>and</u> also whether you would use high or low pressure, in order to favour the production of ammonia in the Haber process. Give reasons for your choice of conditions. (12)

---

11. Answer any **two** of the parts (*a*), (*b*) and (*c*). (2 × 25)

(*a*) The following names are associated with the development of our knowledge of the elements and atomic structure. Choose a name from this list when answering the questions below.

Boyle   **Curie**   **Dalton**   **Mendeleev**   **Rutherford**

(*i*) Who was the Co. Waterford-born scientist who gave us an important gas law and is described as *"the father of modern chemistry"*?

(*ii*) Who was the English schoolteacher who in 1808 described atoms as *"small indivisible particles"*?

(*iii*) Identify the Russian scientist who produced an early version of the periodic table of the elements.

(*iv*) Who was the Polish born scientist who received the Nobel Prize in 1911 for isolating the radioactive elements polonium and radium?

(*v*) Who is credited with the discovery of the nucleus of the atom? (5 × 5)

(*b*) The catalytic converters found in modern cars contain certain metals spread over a fine honeycombed ceramic of very large surface area. Engine exhaust gases react on the surface of the hot solid catalyst to produce less-polluting tailpipe gases.

(*i*) Explain the term *catalyst*.
What term describes the type of catalysis described above? (7)

(*ii*) In the catalytic converter nitrogen monoxide (**NO**) and carbon monoxide (**CO**) react together to give two gaseous products. Identify these two products. (6)

(*iii*) Name **one** of the metals used as a catalyst in the catalytic converter of a car.
Name an element that poisons the catalysts present in a catalytic converter. (12)

(*c*) Answer part **A** *or* part **B**.

A

(*i*) Name the main product of the chemical industry on which you carried out a case study.
What use is made of the product you have named? (10)

(*ii*) Name the principal raw material used in this industry.
Give the source of the raw material you have named. (9)

(*iii*) Is the process by which the product is made a *batch* or a *continuous* process?
Explain your answer. (6)

or

B

In 1964 Dorothy Hodgkin was awarded the Nobel Prize in Chemistry for determining the structures of complex organic molecules.

(*i*) Identify either the vitamin <u>or</u> the antibiotic whose structures were determined by Hodgkin. (4)

Dorothy Hodgkin

(*ii*) What experimental technique did she use to determine these structures? (6)

(*iii*) The father and son team who pioneered this technique are pictured on the right. Who are they? (6)

(*iv*) Give **two** examples of covalent macromolecular solids. (9)

Father & Son

 # Coimisiún na Scrúduithe Stáit
State Examinations Commission

LEAVING CERTIFICATE EXAMINATION, 2007

CHEMISTRY - ORDINARY LEVEL

TUESDAY, 19 JUNE – AFTERNOON 2.00 TO 5.00

400 MARKS

Answer **eight** questions in all

These **must** include at least **two** questions from **Section A**

All questions carry equal marks (50)

Information

Relative atomic masses: $H = 1$, $C = 12$

Molar volume at s.t.p. = 22.4 litres

Avogadro constant = 6×10^{23} mol^{-1}

Section A

Answer at least <u>two</u> questions from this section [see page 1 for full instructions].

1. A group of students prepared a sample of soap in a school laboratory. A mixture of about 4 g of fat, 2 g of sodium hydroxide and 25 cm^3 of ethanol was refluxed for about 30 minutes. The apparatus was then rearranged and the reaction flask heated to remove the ethanol by distillation. Then the residue in the distillation flask was dissolved in a little boiling water and the mixture poured onto brine (saturated sodium chloride solution). The solid soap separated and it was collected by filtration. The soap was washed with a little ice-cold water. Some of the arrangements of apparatus used are drawn on the right.

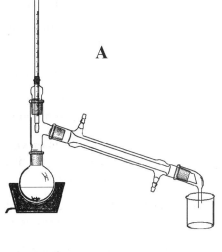

A

(*a*) Which of the arrangements of apparatus (**A** or **B**) was used for
(*i*) the reflux, (*ii*) the distillation stage of the preparation? (8)

(*b*) Draw a rough sketch of either arrangement of apparatus in your answer-book and clearly indicate which part of the condenser should be connected to the cold water tap. (6)

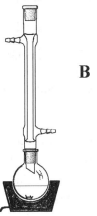

B

(*c*) Why was ethanol added to the fat and the sodium hydroxide? What else should have been added to the reaction flask before heating was commenced? (12)

(*d*) Why was only a small amount of boiling water used to dissolve the residue remaining in the distillation flask after the distillation? (6)

(*e*) When the soap was collected by filtration it was washed with a little ice-cold water.
Why was it important to wash the soap? (6)

(*f*) A small amount of the soap produced in this experiment was added to test tubes containing different water samples and the mixtures were shaken.
What would you expect to observe if the water used was
(*i*) deionised,
(*ii*) from a hard water region? (12)

_____

2. A 0.10 M standard solution of hydrochloric acid (**HCl**) was used to find the concentration of a sodium hydroxide (**NaOH**) solution by titration. The piece of equipment **A** shown in the diagram was used in the experiment.

(*a*) Name the piece of equipment **A**. (5)

(*b*) (*i*) Which of the two solutions is usually measured using the piece of equipment labelled **A**?

    (*ii*) Name the piece of equipment used to measure the second solution used in the titration. (12)

(*c*) (*i*) Describe the correct procedure for rinsing and filling **A**.

    (*ii*) Why is it preferable to use a filler (labelled **B** in the diagram) rather than your mouth when filling **A**?

    (*iii*) State **one** precaution you would take when transferring the liquid measured in **A** to the titration flask to ensure that the correct volume was transferred. (15)

(*d*) Name a suitable indicator for this titration.
What colour change was observed in the titration flask at the end point? (9)

(*e*) The balanced equation for the titration reaction is:

$$HCl \quad + \quad NaOH \quad \rightarrow \quad NaCl \quad + \quad H_2O$$

When the 0.10 M hydrochloric acid solution was titrated a number of times against 25.0 cm³ portions of the sodium hydroxide solution an average accurate titre of 27.5 cm³ was obtained.
Calculate the concentration of the sodium hydroxide solution in moles per litre. (9)

---

3. The apparatus drawn was used in a student experiment to measure the heat of reaction (**ΔH**) for the reaction between 1.0 M hydrochloric acid (**HCl**) solution and 1.0 M sodium hydroxide (**NaOH**) solution. When 50 cm³ of the hydrochloric acid solution was added to 50 cm³ of the sodium hydroxide solution in the polystyrene cup it was found that 2.8 kJ of heat energy was produced by the reaction. The equation for the reaction is:

$$HCl \quad + \quad NaOH \quad \rightarrow \quad NaCl \quad + \quad H_2O$$

(*a*) What is meant by *heat of reaction*? (5)

(*b*) How do the temperature measurements taken during the experiment provide evidence that the reaction between **HCl** and **NaOH** is exothermic? (6)

(*c*) What is the advantage of using a cup made from polystyrene? (6)

(*d*) How would you have obtained a reasonably accurate value for the change in temperature? (9)

(*e*) Calculate   (*i*) the number of moles of hydrochloric acid (**HCl**) in 50 cm³ of 1.0 M hydrochloric acid,

         (*ii*) the heat in kJ which would be produced if a solution containing 1 mole of hydrochloric acid reacted fully with sodium hydroxide,

         (*iii*) the heat of reaction (**ΔH**) for the reaction. (18)

(*f*) What term is used for the reaction between an acid and a base resulting in the production of a salt and water? (6)

Section B

[See page 1 for instructions regarding the number of questions to be answered].

4. Answer **eight** of the following items (*a*), (*b*), (*c*), etc. (50)

   (*a*) State the shape of the water molecule.

   (*b*) What is the mass of 11.2 litres of methane (**CH₄**) gas at s.t.p.?

   (*c*) Give **one** industrial source of hydrogen gas.

   (*d*) Name the piece of equipment used to measure the calorific values of foods.

   (*e*) Write the equilibrium constant (K_c) expression for the following reaction:

   $$N_{2\,(g)} \quad + \quad 3H_{2\,(g)} \quad \rightleftharpoons \quad 2NH_{3\,(g)}$$

   (*f*) Distinguish between *temporary* and *permanent* hardness of water.

   (*g*) A 500 cm³ sample of mineral water has a sodium content of 0.028 g.
   Express the concentration of sodium in parts per million (ppm).

   (*h*) How would you test for the presence of sulfate ions in aqueous solution?

   (*i*) Define *oxidation* in terms of electron transfer.

   (*j*) What *type* of organic reaction is involved in the preparation of ethene from ethanol, represented by the following equation?

   $$C_2H_5OH \quad \rightarrow \quad C_2H_4 \quad + \quad H_2O$$

   (*k*) Answer part **A** or **B**

   A   Give **one** industrial use of nitrogen gas that is based on its lack of chemical reactivity.

   or

   B   Name the process used to recycle scrap iron to produce steel.

   ———————————————

5. (*a*) How many (*i*) protons, (*ii*) neutrons, are there in an atom of potassium-39?
   (*iii*) How are the electrons arranged in shells in this atom?
   (*iv*) What is the valency of potassium? (15)
   [See Mathematics tables p. 44.]

   Litvinenko

   (*b*) In November 2006, a former Soviet agent, Alexander Litvinenko, died in London. The cause of his death was identified as radiation poisoning due to polonium-210.

   (*i*)   Name the French scientist who discovered radioactivity in 1896. (5)

   French scientist

   (*ii*) Name the Polish born scientist who received the Nobel prize in 1911 for the isolation of the radioactive elements polonium and radium. (6)

   (*iii*) Polonium-210 decays with a half-life of 138 days by emitting alpha particles. What is meant by the term *half-life*? What are *alpha particles*? (12)

   Isolated polonium

   (*c*) The scientist shown in the bottom picture discovered the nucleus of the atom by bombarding thin sheets of a particular element with alpha particles from a radioactive source.

   (*i*)   Name this scientist. (6)

   (*ii*) Name the element he bombarded with alpha particles. (6)

   ———————————————

   Discovered nucleus

6. The engines in many modern cars perform well using petrol with an octane number of 95.

$$CH_3 - CH_2 - CH_2 - CH_2 - CH_2 - CH_2 - CH_3$$

A

(a) What do you understand by *octane number*? (8)

(b) The structures of the two compounds (**A** and **B**) on which octane numbers are based are shown on the right. Name the **two** compounds. (12)

$$CH_3 - \overset{\overset{\displaystyle CH_3}{|}}{C} - CH_2 - \overset{\overset{\displaystyle CH_3}{|}}{CH} - CH_3$$
$$\underset{\displaystyle CH_3}{|}$$

B

(c) One of these two compounds is assigned an octane number of 100, and the other an octane number of 0. Which compound is assigned the higher octane number? (6)

(d) Suggest **one** conversion that could be carried out in an oil refinery on the compound of zero octane number in order to produce a compound of higher octane number. (6)

(e) The molecular formula for benzene is C_6H_6. Draw the structure of the molecule. Would you expect the octane number of benzene to be high or low? Give a reason for your answer. (12)

(f) What effects would be noticed when driving a car if the octane number of the petrol used were too low? (6)

---

7. The bond between the chlorine atoms in a chlorine molecule (Cl_2) is a pure (non-polar) covalent bond, whereas the bond between the chlorine atom and the hydrogen atom in the hydrogen chloride molecule (**HCl**) is a polar covalent bond. The bond between chlorine and sodium in sodium chloride (**NaCl**) is an ionic bond.

(a) Define (i) *covalent bond*, (ii) *ionic bond*. (8)

(b) Draw dot and cross diagrams showing the formation of the bonds in (i) Cl_2, (ii) **HCl**, (iii) **NaCl**. (18)

(c) What is meant by a *polar bond*? Explain why the bond in the **HCl** molecule is polar. (9)

(d) Which of the substances, chlorine or sodium chloride, would you expect to be more soluble in water? Give a reason for your answer. (9)

(e) Hydrogen chloride dissolves readily in water to give a solution which is found in gastric juice in the stomach, and which is also commonly used in the school laboratory. Name the solution. (6)

---

8. Answer the questions below with reference to the compounds **A**, **B** and **C**.

C_2H_2	C_2H_4	C_2H_5Cl
A	**B**	**C**

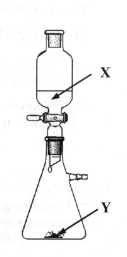

(a) Which one of the three compounds is not a hydrocarbon? (5)

(b) Give the systematic (IUPAC) names of **A**, **B**, and **C**. (9)

(c) Compound **A** can be prepared in the school laboratory by dropping liquid **X** onto solid **Y** using the apparatus shown in the diagram.

   (i) Identify **X** *and* **Y**.

   (ii) Explain, by means of a diagram, how **A** may be collected.

   (iii) Describe how would you show that **A** is unsaturated? (24)

(d) Compound **B** can be easily converted to compound **C**. Identify the reagent used to bring about this conversion *and* state the type of reaction involved. (12)

9. When a hydrogen peroxide (H_2O_2) solution was decomposed in the presence of a suitable catalyst, the oxygen gas produced was collected and its volume measured every three minutes until the reaction was complete. The data obtained is shown in the table.

Time/minutes	0	3	6	9	12	15	18	21
Volume of O_2/cm³	0.0	30	45	53	57	59	60	60

(a) Give the name or formula of a suitable catalyst for this reaction. (5)

(b) Write a balanced equation for the decomposition of hydrogen peroxide (H_2O_2) to form oxygen gas (O_2) and water (H_2O). (6)

(c) Draw a labelled diagram of an apparatus that could be used to carry out this reaction, to collect the oxygen gas, and to measure its volume. (12)

(d) On graph paper, plot a graph of the volume of oxygen gas produced (y-axis) against time (x-axis). (18)

(e) Use your graph to estimate the volume of oxygen gas collected during the first 4.5 minutes. (6)

(f) When this reaction was repeated at a higher temperature it was found that the oxygen gas was produced more quickly. Why does this happen? (3)

_____

10. Answer any **two** of the parts (a), (b) and (c). (2 × 25)

(a) (i)　　Define pH. (7)

(ii)　　Give **two** ways of measuring the pH of a solution. (6)

(iii)　　An aqueous solution has a pH of 7.5 at 25 °C. Is the solution acidic, basic or neutral? (3)

(iv)　　Calculate the pH of a 0.01 M solution of sodium hydroxide. (9)

(b) (i)　　What is *chromatography*? (7)

(ii)　　Describe, with the aid of a diagram, how you would separate the indicators in a mixture of indicators using paper chromatography, thin-layer chromatography or column chromatography. (12)

(iii)　　Which of the three types of chromatography in (ii) above is used in the separation of dyes taken from fibres in forensic work? (6)

(c) The following procedures are involved in the treatment of water for domestic use.

　　　flocculation　　　**filtration**　　　**pH adjustment**　　　**fluoridation**

(i)　　What is meant by flocculation? What substance is added to the water to bring it about? (7)

(ii)　　Outline briefly how the filtration of the water is carried out. What is removed from the water by this procedure? (9)

(iii)　　If the pH of the water were found to be too low, what substance could be added in order to raise it? (3)

(iv)　　How is fluoridation of the water brought about? What is the purpose of fluoridation? (6)

_____

11. Answer any **two** of the parts (*a*), (*b*) and (*c*).　　　　　　　　　　　　　　　　(2 × 25)

(*a*) The following names are associated with the development of our knowledge of elements. Write in your answer-book the omitted name corresponding to each number 1 to 5.

　　　　　　Mendeleev　　　**Dalton**　　　**The Greeks**　　　**Bohr**　　　**Davy**

In ancient times ____1____ suggested that everything that exists was formed from the four elements: earth, air, fire and water. In the early 1800s ____2____ suggested that atoms were tiny indivisible particles. By the use of electrolysis ____3____ isolated elements such as sodium and potassium. By arranging the elements in order of increasing relative atomic mass (atomic weight) and by placing similar elements in groups ____4____ produced a systematic arrangement (an early periodic table) of the elements known to him. From looking at atomic spectra ____5____ came up with the theory that electrons moved around the nucleus of an atom in fixed energy levels (orbits).　　　　(5 × 5)

(*b*) The treatment of sewage can be broken into three stages: **primary**, **secondary** and **tertiary**.

　(*i*)　Which stage involves the biological breakdown of organic matter present in the sewage?　　(6)

　(*ii*)　Which stage involves the screening and settling of the sewage to remove large particles?　　(6)

　(*iii*) Which stage involves the reduction of the levels of nitrates and phosphates?　　(6)

　(*iv*) Why is it important to reduce the levels of nitrates and phosphates in sewage effluent?　　(7)

(*c*) Answer part **A** *or* part **B**.

A

A number of gases present in the lower atmosphere are responsible for the greenhouse effect. This effect is generally beneficial, but it has been increasing in recent times, and this increased greenhouse effect is believed to be responsible for various kinds of damage to the environment.

　(*i*)　What is the *greenhouse effect*?　　(7)

　(*ii*)　Name **two** of the gases responsible for causing the greenhouse effect.　　(6)

　(*iii*) Why is the greenhouse effect largely beneficial?　　(6)

　(*iv*) Give **two** kinds of environmental damage that may result from the increased greenhouse effect.　(6)

　　　　or

B

The diagram shows the electrolysis of molten lead bromide (**PbBr$_2$**) using inert electrodes.

　(*i*)　Suggest a suitable material for the electrodes.　　(7)

　(*ii*)　Identify the product formed at the cathode and also the product formed at the anode.　　(6)

　(*iii*) Why should this electrolysis be carried out in a fume cupboard?　(6)

　(*iv*) Name the pictured English chemist who coined the terms *electrode, electrolysis, anode* and *cathode* in 1832.　　(6)

molten PbBr$_2$

Coimisiún na Scrúduithe Stáit
State Examinations Commission

LEAVING CERTIFICATE EXAMINATION, 2006

CHEMISTRY - ORDINARY LEVEL

TUESDAY, 20 JUNE – AFTERNOON 2.00 TO 5.00

---

400 MARKS

Answer **eight** questions in all

These **must** include at least **two** questions from **Section A**

All questions carry equal marks (50)

Information

Relative atomic masses: H = 1, C = 12, O = 16, Na = 23, Mg = 24, S = 32

Molar volume at s.t.p. = 22.4 litres

Avogadro constant = 6×10^{23} mol^{-1}

Section A

Answer at least <u>two</u> questions from this section [see page 1 for full instructions].

1. Ethene (**C₂H₄**) and ethyne (**C₂H₂**) are *unsaturated* hydrocarbons.
    They can both be easily prepared in a school laboratory.

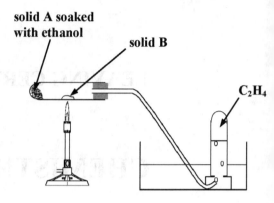

solid A soaked
with ethanol

solid B

C₂H₄

   (*a*) The diagram on the right shows an apparatus which
        could be used for the preparation of ethene gas (**C₂H₄**).

       (*i*)   Identify solid **A** which is used to keep the ethanol
             at the end of the test tube.   (5)

       (*ii*) Give the name <u>or</u> formula of solid **B** which
             is heated using the Bunsen burner.   (6)

       (*iii*) What precaution should be taken when heating
             is stopped? Why is this necessary?   (6)

       (*iv*) Give **one** major use of ethene gas.   (3)

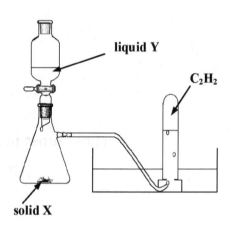

liquid Y

C₂H₂

solid X

   (*b*) The diagram on the right shows an apparatus which
        could be used for the preparation of ethyne gas (**C₂H₂**).

       (*i*)   Identify solid **X** and liquid **Y**, the reagents used in
             the preparation.   (12)

       (*ii*) Describe what you would observe when a sample
             of ethyne gas is burned in air.   (6)

       (*iii*) Give **one** major use of ethyne gas.   (3)

   (*c*) Describe a test you could carry out on either of the two gases to show that it is *unsaturated*.
        What would you observe during the test?   (9)

   _____

2. A 0.06 M *standard solution* of sodium carbonate was made up by weighing out X grams of anhydrous sodium carbonate (Na_2CO_3), dissolving it in deionised water, and making the solution carefully up to the mark in a suitable 1 litre flask. This solution was then used to find, by titration, the concentration of a given hydrochloric acid (HCl) solution. Some of the pieces of equipment used are shown on the right.

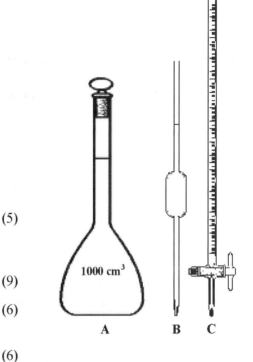

1000 cm³

A   B   C

(a) Name the piece of equipment **A** used to make up 1 litre of the Na_2CO_3 solution.   (5)

(b) What should be done with **A** and its contents immediately after bringing the solution up to the 1 litre mark with deionised water? Why is this important?   (9)

(c) What is meant by a *standard solution*?   (6)

(d) Calculate the mass (X g) of sodium carbonate (Na_2CO_3) required to make 1 litre of a 0.06 M solution.   (6)

(e) Name the pieces of equipment **B** and **C** used in the titration.   (6)

(f) Name a suitable indicator for this titration and state the colour change at the end point.   (6)

(g) What should be done with the conical flask and its contents *during the titration* in order to ensure an accurate result?   (3)

(h) A number of accurate titrations were carried out. It was found that, on average, 25.0 cm³ of the 0.06 M sodium carbonate (Na_2CO_3) solution was neutralised by 30.0 cm³ of the hydrochloric acid (HCl) solution. Calculate the concentration of the hydrochloric acid solution in moles per litre.   (9) The balanced equation for the titration reaction is:

$$Na_2CO_3 \ + \ 2HCl \ \longrightarrow \ 2NaCl \ + \ H_2O \ + \ CO_2$$

---

3. A student was given a bucket of sea water for analysis. The student was asked to find out the concentrations of suspended and dissolved solids in the sea water. The student was also asked to carry out tests to show that the sea water contained sodium ions and chloride ions.

(a) To measure the amount of suspended solids present, the student filtered 500 cm³ of the sea water through a weighed clean dry filter paper. The student then washed the filter paper through with a little distilled water, dried it, and reweighed the filter paper. The filter paper had increased in mass by 0.44 g.

    (i)   Why did the student wash the filter paper with distilled water after filtering the sea water?   (8)

    (ii)   Express the concentration of suspended solids in p.p.m.   (6)

(b) Describe how the student could have then measured the concentration of dissolved solids in the sea water.   (12)

(c) Describe how the student could have carried out a flame test to show that a sodium salt was present in the dissolved solids collected. What flame colour would indicate the presence of sodium ions?   (18)

(d) How could the student have tested the sea water to show that chloride ions were present?   (6)

Section B

[See page 1 for instructions regarding the number of questions to be answered.]

4. Answer **eight** of the following items (*a*), (*b*), (*c*), etc. (50)

   (*a*) The diagram on the right shows the arrangement of electrons in main energy levels (shells) for an atom of a particular element. Identify the element.

   (*b*) What is an *endothermic reaction*?

   (*c*) What is the trend in the size of atomic radii going down any group of the periodic table?

   (*d*) Name the piece of equipment used to measure the calorific values of foods and fuels.

   (*e*) Methylbenzene (toluene) is an aromatic compound of molecular formula C_7H_8. Give its structural formula. State **one** common use of methylbenzene.

   (*f*) Name the English scientist pictured on the right who identified electrons as negatively charged subatomic particles in the 1890s.

   (*g*) Define *oxidation* in terms of electron transfer.

   (*h*) Write the equilibrium constant (K_c) expression for the equilibrium:

   $$2SO_2 \ + \ O_2 \ \rightleftharpoons \ 2SO_3$$

   (*i*) Calculate the percentage by mass of magnesium in magnesium sulfate ($MgSO_4$).

   (*j*) Identify **one** natural product that is extracted by steam distillation.

   (*k*) Answer part **A** *or* part **B**.

   A State **two** ways in which safety can be promoted at a chemical plant.

   or

   B Give any **two** characteristic properties of metals.

---

5. (*a*) Define (*i*) *atomic number*, (*ii*) *relative atomic mass*. (11)

   (*b*) The two best-known isotopes of carbon are carbon-12 and carbon-14.

   (*i*) What term is used in chemistry for the numbers (e.g. 12 and 14 in the case of carbon above) used to identify particular isotopes of an element? (6)

   (*ii*) Name the subatomic particle that is responsible for the difference between carbon-12 and carbon-14. How many of these particles are found in an atom of carbon-14? (6)

   (*iii*) Carbon-14 is radioactive and is an emitter of β-particles (beta-particles). Explain what a β-particle is. Give **one** use of carbon-14. (12)

   (*c*) Define *electronegativity*. (6)

   Use electronegativity values (Mathematics Tables, page 46) to predict the type of bond (ionic, polar covalent or non-polar) likely to be formed between each of the following pairs of elements.

   (*i*) carbon and sulfur, (*ii*) potassium and fluorine, (*iii*) hydrogen and chlorine. (9)

---

6. (a) Hydrocarbons are widely used as fuels.

   (i) What are *hydrocarbons*? Give **one** major source of hydrocarbons. (8)

   (ii) Increasing levels of methane (CH_4) in the lower atmosphere are a concern to environmentalists at present. Explain why this is so. (6)

   (b) Liquid petroleum gas (LPG) is used as a fuel in patio heaters. A major component of LPG includes hydrocarbons of molecular formula C_4H_{10}. Draw the structure and give the systematic (IUPAC) name of each of the **two** structural isomers of C_4H_{10}. (12)

   (c) Words or phrases are omitted from the passage below.

   Write in your answer book suitable words or phrases corresponding to the numbers **1** to **4**.

   To purify a sample of benzoic acid, the impure crystals were dissolved in the ____**1**____ of hot water.

   The hot solution was filtered to remove the ____**2**____ impurities. The filtrate was allowed to cool and,

   when crystals had formed, they were removed from the solution by filtration, leaving the ____**3**____

   impurities behind. This method of purification of a solid is known as ____**4**____. (24)

   _____

7. (a) In 1884, the Swedish chemist, pictured on the right, proposed a new theory of acids and bases. He defined an acid as a substance which produces hydrogen ions (H^+) by dissociation when dissolved in water.

   (i) Identify the Swedish chemist. (5)

   (ii) Define *base* according to the theory proposed by this chemist. (6)

   (iii) Give **one** example of a common household acid and **one** example of a common household base. (6)

   (iv) What do you understand by the term neutralisation? Give **one** everyday example. (9)

   (b) (i) Define pH. (6)

   The concentration of a solution of sodium hydroxide (**NaOH**) is as 4.0 grams per litre.

   (ii) What is the concentration of the solution in moles per litre? (9)

   (iii) Calculate the pH of the solution. (9)

   _____

8. Answer the questions below with reference to compounds **X**, **Y** and **Z** in the following reaction scheme.

$$CH_3CH_2OH \longrightarrow CH_3CHO \longrightarrow CH_3COOH$$
$$\textbf{X} \qquad\qquad \textbf{Y} \qquad\qquad \textbf{Z}$$

   (a) Which **one** of the compounds **X**, **Y** or **Z** has only tetrahedrally bonded carbon atoms? (5)

   (b) Give the names of the compounds **X**, **Y** and **Z**. (9)

   (c) Which of the three compounds **X**, **Y** or **Z** is found

   (i) in concentrations of about 6 – 15% (v/v) in wine,

   (ii) in concentrations of about 6% (v/v) in vinegar? (12)

   (d) Both conversions (**X** to **Y** and **Y** to **Z**) are of the same reaction type.

   (i) What term is used to describe this type of reaction? (18)

   (ii) What reagents could be used to bring about both of these conversions? (18)

   (e) What observation is made when a sample of compound **Y** is heated with Fehling's reagent? (6)

9. (a) The treatment of drinking water for an urban supply consists of a number of stages.
In the case of **any three** of the stages in the treatment process, state the treatment involved and why it is carried out. (20)

(b) The following words all relate to sewage treatment. These words are omitted from the passage below:

  eutrophication nitrates biological sedimentation solid

Write in your answer book the omitted words corresponding to each of the numbers 1 to 5. (30)

In primary treatment, sewage is passed through grids and over grit channels to remove dense ____1____ material. The sewage is then transferred to ____2____ tanks where suspended solids are allowed settle to the bottom. In secondary treatment the sewage is broken down by ____3____ digestion. Tertiary treatment removes phosphates and ____4____. These nutrients can cause ____5____ if their concentrations build up in lakes and rivers.

---

10. Answer any **two** of the parts (a), (b) and (c). (2 × 25)

(a) (i) Describe using a dot and cross diagram the bonding in a molecule of ammonia (**NH₃**). (10)

(ii) What is the shape of the ammonia molecule? (6)

(iii) Would you expect ammonia gas to be soluble or insoluble in water?
Give a reason for your answer. (9)

(b) Mass spectrometry (MS), gas chromatography (GC), high-performance liquid chromatography (HPLC) and thin-layer chromatography (TLC) are all used in analytical chemistry.

(i) Give **one** application of mass spectrometry. (4)

(ii) Give an application of thin-layer chromatography (TLC) in forensic science. (6)

(iii) Give an application of high-performance liquid chromatography (HPLC) in the food industry. (6)

(iv) State the principle on which all chromatographic techniques are based. (9)

(c) Catalysts are used in many important chemical processes. They are used, for example, in the catalytic converters in modern cars.

(i) Explain the term *catalyst*. (4)

(ii) Name **two** of the metals that form the catalyst in the catalytic converter of a car.
What is the advantage of using a catalytic converter? (12)

(iii) Name an element that poisons the catalyst present in a catalytic converter. (3)

(iv) Nitrogen monoxide (**NO**) and carbon monoxide (**CO**) react together in the catalytic converters of modern cars to give two gaseous products. Give the names <u>or</u> formulas of these products. (6)

112

11. Answer any **two** of the parts (*a*), (*b*) and (*c*).   (2 × 25)

(*a*) The diagrams illustrate the arrangement of
      particles in the three states of matter.

 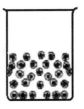 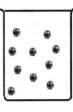

SOLID   **LIQUID**   **GAS**

   (*i*)   Outline briefly the differences between
           the three states in terms of the movement
           of their particles.   (9)

   (*ii*)   What do you understand by *diffusion*?   (6)

   (*iii*) Describe a simple experiment to demonstrate diffusion.   (10)

(*b*) Define *rate of reaction*.   (7)

The effect of concentration on reaction rate can be studied using the
reaction between sodium thiosulfate solution and hydrochloric acid.
The apparatus shown in the diagram may be used. As the reaction
proceeds, the reaction mixture becomes cloudy and, after a certain
time, the cross becomes invisible when viewed through the solution.
The equation for the reaction is

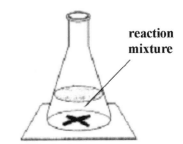

reaction mixture

$$Na_2S_2O_3 + 2HCl \rightarrow 2NaCl + H_2O + SO_2 + S$$

   (*i*)   Which product of the reaction causes the reaction mixture to become cloudy?   (6)

   (*ii*)   If a higher concentration of sodium thiosulfate solution were used in the reaction, would the time
           taken for the cross to become invisible be greater, less or unchanged? Explain your answer.   (6)

   (*iii*) If the conical flask were surrounded by ice-water, would the time taken for the cross to become
           invisible be greater, less or unchanged? Explain your answer.   (6)

(*c*) Answer part **A** *or* part **B**.

   A

   (*i*)   Explain the term *feedstock* in industrial chemistry.   (7)

   In planning to set up a chemical factory, finding a suitable location and the minimisation
   of costs, both fixed and variable, are very important considerations.

   (*ii*)   State any **two** factors that would influence the choice of location for the factory.   (6)

   (*iii*) Explain the difference between fixed costs and variable costs by giving **one** example
           in each case.   (6)

   (*iv*)   Name **two** important products of the Irish chemical industry.   (6)

                                              or

   B

   Poly(phenylethene), also known as polystyrene, is a widely-used addition <u>polymer</u>.

   (*i*)   Explain the underlined term.   (7)

   (*ii*)   Give any **two** common uses of poly(phenylethene).   (6)

   (*iii*) State any **two** of the procedures involved in the recycling of poly(phenylethene)   (6)

   (*iv*)   Name **one** other addition polymer.   (6)

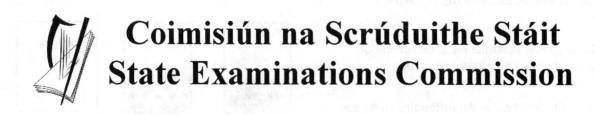

Coimisiún na Scrúduithe Stáit
State Examinations Commission

LEAVING CERTIFICATE EXAMINATION, 2005

CHEMISTRY - ORDINARY LEVEL

TUESDAY, 21 JUNE – AFTERNOON 2.00 TO 5.00

---

400 MARKS

Answer **eight** questions in all

These **must** include at least **two** questions from **Section A**

All questions carry equal marks (50)

Information

Relative atomic masses: H = 1, Cl = 35.5

Molar volume at s.t.p. = 22.4 litres

Avogadro constant = $6 \times 10^{23} \, \text{mol}^{-1}$

Section A

Answer at least <u>two</u> questions from this section [see page 1 for full instructions].

1. A group of students prepared ethanal (**CH₃CHO**) by slowly adding a mixture of ethanol (**C₂H₅OH**) and an oxidising agent in water, to hot aqueous sulfuric acid. The apparatus drawn below was used.

(*a*) At the start of the experiment a few pieces of a solid material were placed in the reaction flask along with the sulfuric acid. Identify this solid and state its purpose. (8)

(*b*) Identify a suitable oxidising agent for this preparation. (6)

(*c*) What is the colour of the mixture in the dropping funnel at the start? (6)

(*d*) What is the colour of the mixture in the reaction flask as the reaction proceeds? (6)

(*e*) Why is it important to distill off the ethanal as it is produced? (6)

(*f*) Why is it not necessary to keep heating the reaction flask during the addition? (6)

(*g*) Why is the receiving vessel cooled in ice-water? (6)

(*h*) What colour is the solid produced when a mixture containing a few drops of Fehling's solutions (No 1 and No 2) and ethanal is heated? (6)

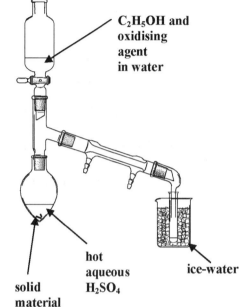

C₂H₅OH and oxidising agent in water

hot aqueous H₂SO₄

ice-water

solid material

---

2. A 0.10 M standard solution of sodium hydroxide (**NaOH**) was used to find the concentration of a given hydrochloric acid (**HCl**) solution by titration. The pieces of equipment **A** and **B** shown in the diagram were used in the experiment.

(*a*) Name the pieces of equipment **A** and **B**. (8)

(*b*) Which of the two solutions is normally placed in the piece of equipment labelled **A**?
Describe the correct procedure for rinsing and filling **A**. (12)

(*c*) Name a suitable indicator for this titration.
What colour change was observed at the end point? (9)

(*d*) The balanced equation for the titration reaction is:

$$NaOH + HCl \rightarrow NaCl + H_2O$$

When the hydrochloric acid (**HCl**) solution was titrated a number of times against 25 cm³ portions of the 0.10 M solution of sodium hydroxide (**NaOH**), an average accurate titre of 22.6 cm³ was obtained.

Calculate the concentration of the hydrochloric acid solution in moles per litre. (9)

A   B

(*e*) Describe how this experiment could be used to prepare a pure sample of sodium chloride (common salt). (12)

---

3. Hydrogen peroxide solution decomposes rapidly in the presence of a suitable catalyst according to the following equation.

$$2H_2O_2 \quad \rightarrow \quad 2H_2O \quad + \quad O_2$$

In an experiment using this reaction, the oxygen gas was collected and its volume measured every two minutes until the reaction was complete. The data obtained is shown in the table.

Time/minutes	0	2	4	6	8	10	12	14	16
Volume of O_2/cm^3	0.0	31	55	74	87	95	99	100	100

(a) What is a *catalyst*? Name a suitable catalyst for this reaction. (8)

(b) Draw a labelled diagram of an apparatus which could be used to carry out this reaction, collect the oxygen gas, and measure its volume. (12)

(c) On graph paper, plot a graph of the volume of oxygen gas produced (*y*-axis) against time (*x*-axis). (18)

(d) Why does the rate of oxygen production decrease as time passes? (6)

(e) Use the graph to estimate the volume of oxygen gas collected during the first 3 minutes. (6)

Section B

[See page 1 for instructions regarding the number of questions to be answered]

4. Answer **eight** of the following items (*a*), (*b*), (*c*), etc. (50)

   (*a*) Name the Russian scientist pictured on the right who proposed an early version of the periodic table in 1867.

   (*b*) Describe the nature (composition) of an alpha-particle (α-particle).

   (*c*) Define *electronegativity*.

   (*d*) Name the piece of equipment used to measure the calorific value of foods and fuels.

   (*e*) Give the name or formula of the acid which is the cause of the sting of nettles.

   (*f*) A 500 cm^3 bottle of mineral water contains 0.480 g of dissolved solids. Calculate the concentration of dissolved solids in p.p.m.

   (*g*) Write the arrangement of the electrons in the main energy levels of a calcium atom.

   (*h*) The label on a bottle of whiskey says that the alcohol content is 40% (v/v). How many cm^3 of ethanol are there in 30 cm^3 of the whiskey?

   (*i*) Write the equilibrium constant (K_c) expression for the equilibrium:

   $$3H_2 \ + \ N_2 \ \rightleftharpoons \ 2NH_3$$

   (*j*) Define *reduction* in terms of electron transfer.

   (*k*) Answer part **A** or **B**

   A   What is the chemical formula for ozone? State **one** beneficial effect of the ozone layer.

   or

   B   State **two** general chemical properties of transition metals.

   _____

5. Each of the following were important contributors to what we know about atomic structure, the elements or radioactivity.

   Bohr   Becquerel   Curie   Dalton   The Greeks   Moseley   Thomson   Rutherford

   Select from the list above one answer to each of the following.

   (*a*) Who proposed the early theory that matter consists of the four elements: earth, air, fire and water? (7)

   (*b*) Who described atoms as small indivisible particles? (7)

   (*c*) Who identified electrons as sub-atomic particles? (6)

   (*d*) Who is credited with the discovery of the nucleus of the atom? (6)

   (*e*) Who proposed a model for the atom in which the electrons circulated around the nucleus in fixed energy levels or orbits? (6)

   (*f*) Who discovered that uranium salts emitted radiation? (6)

   (*g*) Who received a Nobel Prize for the isolation of the elements polonium and radium? (6)

   (*h*) Whose determination of the charge on the nucleus of atoms allowed the systematic arrangement of the elements in the modern periodic table? (6)

   _____

6. (*a*) Alkynes form a *homologous series* of which ethyne (C_2H_2) is the first member.

      (*i*)   What is a *homologous series*? (5)

      (*ii*) Draw the structure of the ethyne molecule. (6)

      (*iii*) In a chemical reaction, three molecules of ethyne can combine to form an aromatic molecule of formula C_6H_6. Give the name *or* structure of this molecule. (6)

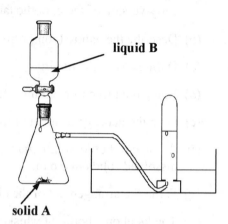

liquid B

(*b*) The diagram on the right shows an apparatus which could be used for the preparation of ethyne gas.

      (*i*)   Identify the solid **A** and the liquid **B** used in the preparation. (12)

      (*ii*) Describe what you would observe when a sample of ethyne gas is burned in air. (6)

      (*iii*) Describe a test you could carry out on a sample of ethyne gas to show that the gas is unsaturated. (9)

      (*iv*) Give **one** major use of ethyne gas. (6)

solid A

---

7. (*a*) What is meant by (*i*) an *ionic bond*, (*ii*) a *covalent bond*? (8)

(*b*) Describe using dot and cross diagrams the bond formation in

      (*i*) water (H_2O), (*ii*) sodium chloride ($NaCl$). (18)

(*c*) What is the shape of the water molecule? (6)

(*d*) What colour would a sample of sodium chloride impart to a Bunsen flame? (6)

(*e*) The diagram shows a thin stream of water flowing from a suitable piece of equipment. What would be observed if a charged rod was held close to the stream of water?
What property of water does this experiment demonstrate? (12)

---

8. Examine the reaction scheme and answer the questions that follow:

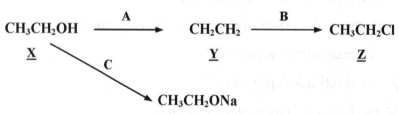

(*a*) Which **one** of the compounds <u>X</u>, <u>Y</u> or <u>Z</u> is an unsaturated hydrocarbon? (5)

(*b*) Name the compound <u>Y</u>. (6)

(*c*) Classify (*i*) conversion **A**, (*ii*) conversion **B**, as an *addition*, an *elimination* or a *substitution* reaction. (12)

(*d*) Draw a clearly labelled diagram of the apparatus used to carry out conversion **A** in a school laboratory.

Identify the compound used to bring about this conversion. (15)

(*e*) What reagent is used to bring about (*i*) conversion **B**, (*ii*) conversion **C**? (12)

9. (*a*) The following words all refer to stages in water treatment. These words are omitted from the passage below:

chlorination	**filtration**	**flocculation**
pH adjustment	**fluoridation**	**sedimentation**

Write in your answer book the omitted words corresponding to each of the numbers 1 to 6. (36)

Aluminium sulfate and/or a polyelectrolyte is added to water to help suspended solids clump together in a process called ____1____. Following this addition the suspended solids are allowed settle to the bottom of ____2____ tanks. Bacteria in the water are destroyed by ____3____. Lime or acid is added to carry out ____4____. In Ireland ____5____ of water is carried out in urban supplies to help prevent tooth decay. The water is passed through beds of sand and gravel to remove any remaining suspended solids in a process called ____6____.

(*b*) Identify **two** substances removed by the tertiary treatment of sewage effluent.
State **one** damaging environmental effect of these substances. (14)

---

10. Answer any **two** of the parts (*a*), (*b*) and (*c*). (2×25)

(*a*) The diagram shows a fractionation tower of an oil refinery. The main fractions produced are named.

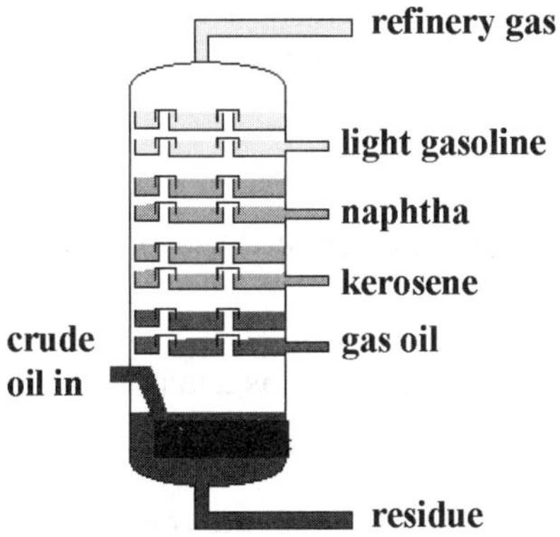

(*i*) Which fraction is used as tar or bitumen in surfacing roads? (7)

(*ii*) Identify the fraction which is rich in propane and butane, and which is used as a fuel for outdoor (space) heaters? (6)

(*iii*) Which fraction is used as an aircraft fuel? (6)

(*iv*) Which fraction is a heavy fuel oil used in furnaces? (6)

refinery gas
light gasoline
naphtha
kerosene
crude oil in
gas oil
residue

(*b*) (*i*) Define *pH*. (7)

The concentration of a solution of hydrochloric acid (**HCl**) is given as 3.65 grams per litre.

(*ii*) What is the concentration of the solution in moles per litre? (9)

(*iii*) Calculate the pH of the solution. (9)

(*c*) It is possible to estimate the *free chlorine* in swimming pool water or bleach using a colorimeter or a comparator.

(*i*) Describe how you could measure the free chlorine in either swimming pool water or bleach using one of these methods. (18)

(*ii*) Outline briefly the principles on which the technique you have described in (*i*) is based. (7)

119

11. Answer any **two** of the parts (*a*), (*b*) and (*c*).   (2 × 25)

(*a*) Paper chromatography, thin-layer chromatography and column chromatography are all separation techniques.

   (*i*)   Describe with the aid of a diagram an experiment to separate a mixture of indicators using **one** of these techniques.   (15)

   (*ii*) What material is the stationary phase in the experiment you have described?   (5)

   (*iii*) Give **one** example of the use of thin-layer chromatography in forensic science.   (5)

(*b*) The diagram shows an arrangement for the electrolysis of copper(II) sulfate solution using copper electrodes.

   (*i*)   Write the chemical formula for copper(II) sulfate.
           What colour is the copper(II) sulfate solution?   (7)

   (*ii*) State **one** change which happens to the electrode labelled **A** during the experiment.   (6)

   (*iii*) If you wished to electroplate a metal object with copper, which of the electrodes, **A** or **B**, should be replaced by the object?   (6)

   (*iv*) If you wished to purify a sample of copper, which of the electrodes, **A** or **B**, should you replace with the piece of impure copper?   (6)

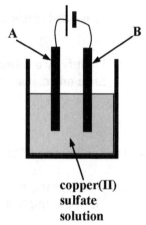

copper(II) sulfate solution

(*c*) Answer part **A** *or* part **B**.

   A

   Air serves as a major source of both nitrogen gas and oxygen gas.

   (*i*)   How is oxygen gas produced commercially from air?   (4)

   (*ii*) State **one** commercial use of oxygen and **one** commercial use of nitrogen.   (6)

   (*iii*) What is meant by *nitrogen fixation*? Why is it important?   (9)

   (*iv*) Give **one** way in which nitrogen is fixed in nature.   (6)

or

   B

   (*i*)   Name the English scientist pictured on the right who isolated the elements sodium and potassium in the early 1800s.   (4)

   (*ii*) Both sodium and potassium *corrode* easily. What is meant by *corrosion*?   (6)

   The corrosion of iron can be prevented by *galvanising*.

   (*iii*) How is a piece of iron galvanised?   (6)

   (*iv*) How does this prevent the iron from corroding?   (6)

   (*v*)   State **one** method, other than galvanising, which helps prevent iron from corroding.   (3)

English scientist who isolated sodium and potassium in the early 1800s

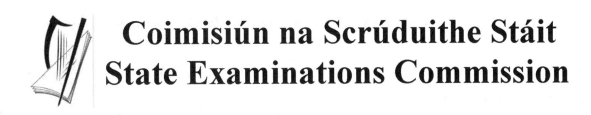

Coimisiún na Scrúduithe Stáit
State Examinations Commission

LEAVING CERTIFICATE EXAMINATION, 2004

CHEMISTRY - ORDINARY LEVEL

TUESDAY, 22 JUNE – AFTERNOON 2.00 TO 5.00

---

400 MARKS

Answer **eight** questions in all

These **must** include at least **two** questions from **Section A**

All questions carry equal marks (50)

Information

Relative atomic masses: H = 1, O = 16, S = 32

Molar volume at s.t.p. = 22.4 litres

Avogadro constant = 6×10^{23} mol^{-1}

Section A

Answer at least <u>two</u> questions from this section [see page 1 for full instructions].

1. The apparatus shown in the diagram was used to prepare a sample of ethene gas (C_2H_4). A little of liquid **X** was poured into a boiling tube and some glass wool was pushed to the end of the boiling tube. Some powdered solid **Y** was heaped about halfway along the tube. A Bunsen flame was used to heat the outside of the boiling tube under **Y**. A number of test tubes of gas were collected.

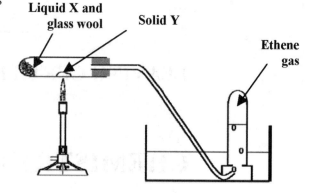

(a) Identify the liquid **X** and the solid **Y**. (8)
   What is the colour of solid **Y**? (3)

(b) What is the purpose of the glass wool? (6)

(c) Why were the first few test tubes of gas collected not used? (6)

(d) When heating is stopped at the end of the experiment a suck back of water into the boiling tube is likely to occur. Why might a suck back occur when the heating is stopped, and what action should be taken to avoid this happening? (9)

(e) Describe a laboratory test you could carry out on a test tube of ethene to show combustion of the gas. What is observed during this test? What are the products of the combustion reaction? Describe a test to confirm the presence of **one** of these combustion products. (18)

_____

2. A 0.10 M standard solution of sodium carbonate (Na_2CO_3) was used to find the concentration of a given hydrochloric acid solution by titration. The pieces of apparatus **A**, **B**, **C** and **D** shown in the diagram were used in the experiment.

(a) Name the pieces of apparatus **A**, **B**, and **C**. (11)

(b) Describe the correct procedure for rinsing **A** before using it to measure the sodium carbonate solution. (6)

(c) Mention **two** precautions which should be taken when using **B**. (9)

(d) **D** is a wash bottle containing deionised water. What use should be made of it *during* the titration? (6)

(e) Name a suitable indicator for this titration. What colour change was observed in **C** at the end point? (9)

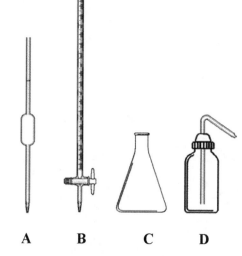

A   **B**   **C**   **D**

(f) The balanced equation for the titration reaction is:

$$Na_2CO_3 + 2HCl \rightarrow 2NaCl + H_2O + CO_2$$

When the hydrochloric acid (**HCl**) solution was titrated a number of times against 25 cm³ portions of the 0.10 M solution of sodium carbonate (Na_2CO_3) an average accurate titre of 20.0 cm³ was obtained. Calculate the concentration of the hydrochloric acid solution in moles per litre. (9)

_____

3. The diagram shows an apparatus used to measure the heat of reaction (ΔH) for the reaction between hydrochloric acid (**HCl**) and a solution of sodium hydroxide (**NaOH**).

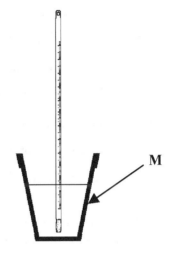

(a) The reaction occurring in this experiment is *exothermic*. Explain the term *exothermic*. (5)

(b) Name a suitable material for container **M**. Explain your choice of material. (12)

(c) Name a piece of apparatus which could have been used in this experiment to measure out 100 cm³ of hydrochloric acid solution accurately. (3)

(d) State **one** precaution which could have been taken to obtain an accurate value for the final temperature reached when the two solutions were mixed. (6)

(e) Both hydrochloric acid and sodium hydroxide solutions are corrosive. Describe <u>or</u> draw a clear diagram of the hazard-warning symbol that should be used on the labels of bottles to indicate that the contents are corrosive. (6)

(f) When 100 cm³ of 1.0 M hydrochloric acid reacted with excess sodium hydroxide solution, 5.71 kJ of heat were produced.

    (i)   How many moles of hydrochloric acid reacted?
    (ii)   How many kJ of heat would have been produced if one mole of hydrochloric acid (**HCl**) reacted?
    (iii) Hydrochloric acid reacts with sodium hydroxide according to the equation:

$$\text{HCl} \;+\; \text{NaOH} \;\rightarrow\; \text{NaCl} \;+\; \text{H}_2\text{O}$$

What is the heat of reaction (ΔH) for the reaction between hydrochloric acid and sodium hydroxide? (12)

(g) The energy content (calorific value) of foods and fuels can be measured in a special piece of apparatus. Name this apparatus. (6)

Section B

[See page 1 for instructions regarding the number of questions to be answered]

4. Answer **eight** of the following items (*a*), (*b*), (*c*), etc. (50)

   (*a*) Name the scientist who discovered the nucleus of the atom.

   (*b*) State **one** use of the radioisotope ^{60}Co (cobalt-60).

   (*c*) What is the trend in the size of atomic radii across a period of the periodic table?

   (*d*) State **two** characteristic properties of ionic substances.

   (*e*) What is the volume in litres of 6×10^{23} gaseous molecules at standard temperature and pressure?

   (*f*) Write the name <u>or</u> formula of the carboxylic acid found in vinegar.

   (*g*) The label on a bottle of wine says that the alcohol content is 11% (v/v). How many cm^3 of ethanol per litre does this wine contain?

   (*h*) A 100 cm^3 sample of sea water contained 0.022 grams of suspended solids. Calculate the concentration of suspended solids in p.p.m.

   (*i*) Write the equilibrium constant expression (K_c) for the equilibrium

$$2SO_2 \ + \ O_2 \ \rightleftharpoons \ 2SO_3$$

   (*j*) Why is chlorine added to domestic water supplies?

   (*k*) Answer part **A** <u>or</u> **B**

   A   State **two** factors used to determine choice of location for a chemical industry.

or

   B   Use a suitable example to explain the term alloy.

———————————————

5. (*a*) The following words are omitted from the passage below:

electronegativity	polar	pair
water	non-polar	boiling points

Write in your answer book the omitted words corresponding to each of the numbers 1 to 6. (36)

A covalent bond is formed when a _____1_____ of electrons is shared between the bonding atoms.

When the electrons are shared equally, a _____2_____ covalent bond is formed, but when one atom has a greater attraction for the bonding electrons, a _____3_____ covalent bond is formed. Most covalent compounds have low _____4_____ and do not dissolve very well in _____5_____. The nature of chemical bonds can be predicted using _____6_____ values.

   (*b*) Draw a dot and cross diagram to describe the bonding in methane (CH_4). (9)

   What is the shape of the methane molecule? (5)

———————————————

6. The following compounds are all used as fuels:

methane   **butane**   **benzene**   **ethyne**   **hydrogen**

(a) Select from the list above one compound in each case which

    (i)   is often formed in refuse dumps and slurry pits, (5)

    (ii)   is used in oxyacetylene torches for cutting and welding, (6)

    (iii) is used as a fuel for space rockets, (6)

    (iv) is a component of liquid petroleum gas (LPG), (6)

    (v)   has a high octane number. (6)

(b) One of the compounds listed above is described as *aromatic*. Which compound is *aromatic*? Draw a diagram to show the structure of a molecule of this compound. (12)

(c) Give **one** disadvantage of hydrogen as a fuel. (3)
State **one** method of manufacturing hydrogen gas on an industrial scale. (6)

---

7. Hydrogen peroxide solution decomposes rapidly in the presence of a manganese dioxide catalyst according to the following equation.

$$2H_2O_2 \rightarrow 2H_2O + O_2$$

In an experiment using this reaction, the oxygen gas was collected and its volume measured every minute until the reaction was complete. The data obtained is shown in the table.

Time/minutes	0	1	2	3	4	5	6	7	8
Volume of O_2/cm^3	0.0	7.7	11.7	14.8	17.2	19.0	19.8	20.0	20.0

(a) Draw a labelled diagram of the apparatus which could be used to carry out this reaction, collect the oxygen gas, and measure its volume. (11)

(b) On graph paper, plot a graph of the volume of oxygen gas produced (*y*-axis) against time (*x*-axis). (18)

(c) Was the rate of reaction faster after 1 minute or after 4 minutes? Explain your answer, referring to the shape of your graph in doing so. (6)

(d) Use the graph to estimate the volume of oxygen gas collected after 2.5 minutes. (9)

(e) Use the graph to estimate the time at which the reaction was complete. (6)

---

8. Examine the reaction scheme and answer the questions that follow:

$$\underset{\underline{\textbf{A}}}{CH_2CH_2} \overset{\textbf{X}}{\rightarrow} \underset{\underline{\textbf{B}}}{CH_3CH_3} \overset{\textbf{Y}}{\rightarrow} \underset{\underline{\textbf{C}}}{CH_3CH_2Cl}$$

(a) Which **one** of the compounds **A**, **B** or **C** is an unsaturated hydrocarbon? (5)

(b) Which **one** of the compounds **A**, **B** or **C** has only planar carbon atoms? (6)

(c) Name the compounds **A**, **B** and **C**. (18)

(d) Classify (i) conversion **X** and (ii) conversion **Y** as an *addition, elimination* or *substitution* reaction. (12)

(e) Which **one** of the compounds **A**, **B** or **C** is easily polymerised? State the name of the polymer formed. (9)

---

9. (a) What is meant by the term *hard water*? (5)

How may *temporary* hardness be removed from a water sample? (6)

Give the name **and** formula of a compound which causes *permanent* hardness in water (9)

(b) Select from the following list the answers to the questions labelled (i) to (v) below.

eutrophication　　　　**bacterial breakdown**

phosphates and nitrates　　**settlement and screening**　　**silage effluent**

(i) What takes place in the primary treatment of sewage?

(ii) What process occurs in the secondary treatment of sewage?

(iii) What does tertiary treatment of sewage remove?

(iv) Which term describes the enrichment of water with nutrients?

(v) Name a pollutant which can cause the enrichment of water with nutrients. (30)

---

10. Answer any **two** of the parts (a), (b) and (c). (2×25)

(a) Define the terms (i) *acid*, (ii) *base* and (iii) *neutralisation*. (13)

Give an everyday example of neutralisation. (6)

Name a household base. (6)

(b) Define *relative atomic mass*. (7)

Calculate the relative molecular mass of sulfuric acid (H_2SO_4) from the relative atomic masses of its elements. (6)

What is the percentage by mass of sulfur in sulfuric acid? (9)

How many moles of sulfuric acid are contained in 4.9 g of the acid? (3)

(c) Protons, neutrons and electrons are located in the atom.
Copy the table below into your answer book and fill in the missing information. (13)

	Relative mass	Relative charge	Location
Proton	1		
Electron	1/1840		Outside the nucleus
Neutron		0	In the nucleus

Define *atomic number*. (6)

State the arrangement of electrons in the main energy levels in an atom of potassium. (6)

---

11. Answer any **two** of the parts (*a*), (*b*) and (*c*).   (2 × 25)

(*a*) Define *oxidation* in terms of electron transfer.   (7)

When zinc is added to copper sulfate solution the copper is displaced according to the equation:

$$\textbf{Zn} \ + \ \textbf{CuSO}_4 \ \rightarrow \ \textbf{Cu} \ + \ \textbf{ZnSO}_4$$

   (*i*)   State **one** change observed as the reaction proceeds.   (6)

   (*ii*) Which substance is oxidised?   (6)

   (*iii*) Scrap iron can be used to extract copper metal. Which of these two metals is higher up the
           electrochemical series?   (6)

(*b*) Define pH.   (7)

Describe how you would use universal indicator paper (pH paper) or solution to measure the pH of a
river water sample.   (9)

Calculate the pH of a 0.001 M solution of nitric acid (**HNO₃**).   (9)

(*c*) Answer part **A** *or* part **B**.

   A

   Explain the terms (*i*) *feedstock* and (*ii*) *co-products* as used in industrial chemistry.   (10)

   Explain how batch and continuous processes differ.   (9)

   Specify **two** ways in which the chemical industry has made a positive contribution to modern life. (6)

or

   B

   Name the father and son team pictured on the right who
   were pioneers in the study of X-ray crystallography.   (5)

**Pioneers in the study of
X-ray crystallography**

   Copy the table into your answer book and fill in the missing
   information about the binding forces in each crystal.   (15)

Type of crystal	Example	Binding Forces
Ionic	Sodium chloride	
Molecular	Iodine	
Covalent macromolecular	Diamond	

   Name the scientist pictured on the right who determined
   the crystal structures of vitamin B₁₂ and penicillin.   (5)

**The scientist who determined the
structures of vitamin B₁₂ and penicillin**

Coimisiún na Scrúduithe Stáit
State Examinations Commission

LEAVING CERTIFICATE EXAMINATION, 2003

CHEMISTRY - ORDINARY LEVEL

TUESDAY, 17 JUNE - AFTERNOON 2.00 to 5.00

400 MARKS

Answer **eight** questions in all

These **must** include at least **two** questions from **Section A**

All questions carry equal marks (50)

Information

Relative atomic masses: H = 1, C = 12, O = 16, Na = 23, Mg = 24, Ca = 40

Molar volume at s.t.p. = 22.4 l

Avogadro constant = 6×10^{23} mol^{-1}

Section A

Answer at least <u>two</u> questions from this section [see page 1 for full instructions]

1. The diagram shows an apparatus that can be used for the preparation of ethyne gas, C_2H_2.

   A liquid **X** is dropped onto the solid **Y** and the gas collected in test tubes as shown. The first few test tubes of gas collected are not usually used.

   (a) Name the piece of equipment, **A**, from which the liquid **X** is added. (5)

   (b) Identify the liquid **X** and the solid **Y**. (12)

   (c) Describe the appearance of the solid **Y**. (3)

   (d) Why are the first few test tubes of gas collected not usually used? (6)

   (e) What is observed when a sample of ethyne gas is burned in air? (6)

   (f) To what family of compounds (homologous series) does ethyne belong? (6)

   (g) Ethyne is a *hydrocarbon*. What is meant by the term *hydrocarbon*? (6)

   (h) The common name for ethyne is acetylene. Give **one** use of this gas. (6)

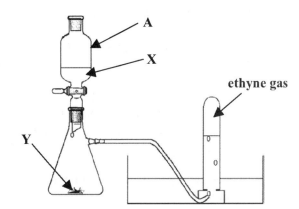

2. To prepare 500 cm³ of a standard solution of sodium carbonate, **Na₂CO₃**, 2.65 g of solid anhydrous sodium carbonate, was weighed on a clock glass using an electronic balance. All of the solid was then carefully transferred from the clock glass into a beaker and a small amount of deionised water was added. When the solid was dissolved the solution was transferred to a 500 cm³ volumetric flask and deionised water added until the bottom of the meniscus was level with the mark. The volumetric flask was then stoppered and inverted several times. Some of the pieces of equipment used are drawn on the right.

(*a*) What is meant by a *standard solution*?   (5)

(*b*) Name the pieces of equipment **A, B, C** and **D**.   (12)

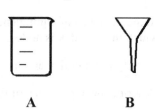

A   **B**

(*c*) Why was it important to transfer all of the solid from the clock glass to the beaker? What could you do to insure all the solid was transferred?   (9)

(*d*) Why was <u>deionised</u> water used to make up the solution?   (6)

(*e*) Why was the volumetric flask stoppered and inverted several times at the end?   (6)

(*f*) The solution contained 2.65 g of anhydrous sodium carbonate, **Na₂CO₃**, in 500 cm³ of solution. Calculate the concentration of the solution in moles per litre.   (12)

C   **D**

---

3. Flame tests can be used to identify metallic elements present in salts.

(*a*) Copy and complete the table below into your answer book matching the following flame colours with the correct metallic elements.   (14)

orange-yellow   lilac   green   crimson-red

METAL	Lithium (Li)	Sodium (Na)	Potassium (K)	Copper (Cu)
FLAME COLOUR				

(*b*) Describe how you would carry out a flame test on a sample of sodium sulfate.   (18)

(*c*) Outside a science laboratory where would you expect to find lights containing sodium vapour?   (6)

(*d*) Describe a test to confirm the presence of sulfate ions in aqueous solution.   (12)

Section B

[See page 1 for instructions regarding the number of questions to be answered]

4. Answer **eight** of the following items (*a*), (*b*), (*c*), etc. (50)

   (*a*) How many (*i*) protons and (*ii*) neutrons has $^{37}_{17}Cl$?

   (*b*) State *Le Chatelier's principle*.

   (*c*) What is the shape of the methane, **CH₄**, molecule?

   (*d*) List the following three types of radiation in order of <u>decreasing</u> penetrating power

alpha- (α-)	**beta- (β-)**	**gamma- (γ-)**

   (*e*) Write a balanced chemical equation for the combustion of methane, **CH₄**, in oxygen.

   (*f*) What is the percentage by mass of carbon in calcium carbonate, **CaCO₃**?

   (*g*) Define the term *relative atomic mass*.

   (*h*) Calculate the pH of a 0.01 M solution of hydrochloric acid, **HCl**.

   (*i*) The famous Irish scientist shown on the right, was born in 1627. He was a son of the Earl of Cork. His name is associated with a gas law. Name him.

   (*j*) Write the equilibrium constant expression, K_c, for the equilibrium

   $$H_2 \;+\; I_2 \rightleftharpoons\; 2HI$$

   (*k*) Answer part **A** <u>or</u> **B**

   A   How does *nitrogen fixation* occur in nature?

   or

   B   What is meant by the *corrosion of metals?*

---

5. (*a*) Mendeleev was one of the first scientists to produce a periodic table of the elements.

   (*i*) How were the elements arranged in Mendeleev's periodic table? (8)

   (*ii*) State **two** differences between the way in which Mendeleev arranged the elements in his periodic table and the way in which the elements are arranged in the modern periodic table. (12)

   (*b*) Match the following scientists with the statements (*i*) to (*v*) below. (30)

Thomson	**Curie**	**Rutherford**	**Bohr**	**Dalton**

   (*i*) The scientist who said that atoms were indivisible

   (*ii*) The scientist who discovered the nucleus of the atom

   (*iii*) The scientist who discovered the radioactive elements polonium and radium

   (*iv*) The scientist who discovered that electrons were sub-atomic particles

   (*v*) The scientist who proposed a model for the atom which stated that electrons travel around the nucleus in fixed energy levels or shells.

---

6. The fractional distillation of crude oil in an oil refinery produced the following fractions:

gas   naphtha   kerosene   gas oil   residue

(a) Select from the list the fraction which is the main fraction used to make petrol.   (5)

The hydrocarbons present in the fraction that is used to make petrol usually have a low *octane rating*.

   (i)   What is meant by the term *octane rating*?   (6)

   (ii)   Name the heavy metal that was commonly used in compounds that were added to petrol to increase its octane rating? Why was its use discontinued?   (12)

   (iii)   Name a chemical process that is now used to increase the octane rating of petrol.   (6)

(b) Select from the list above the fraction

   (i)   which is used as an aircraft fuel

   (ii)   which is used as "tar" or "bitumen" in surfacing roads.   (12)

(c) Select from the list the fraction which is used as a heavy fuel oil for furnaces and which was spilled in large quantities from the oil tanker the "Prestige" causing major environmental damage on the coast of Spain in November 2002. State **one** of the types of environmental damage done by this spillage.   (9)

---

7. (a) Define *electronegativity*.   (8)

Describe using dot and cross diagrams the bonding in

   (i)   sodium chloride, **NaCl**,   (ii)   hydrogen chloride, **HCl**.   (18)

Which of these two substances would you expect to have the higher melting point?
Give a reason for your answer.   (6)

(b) Define *oxidation* in terms of electron transfer.   (6)

In the reaction of sodium with chlorine to produce sodium chloride which element is reduced?
Explain your answer.   (12)

---

8. Examine the reaction scheme and answer the questions which follow:

$$C_2H_5OH \xrightarrow{\text{X}} CH_2CH_2 \xrightarrow{\text{Y}} CH_2BrCH_2Br$$

     A   **B**   **C**

(a) Which of the compounds **A**, **B** or **C** can be polymerised to make the plastic used in plastic bags and milk crates?   (5)

(b) Classify the conversions **X** and **Y** as *addition, elimination* or *substitution* reactions.   (12)

(c) Name the compounds **A**, **B** and **C**.   (18)

(d) The apparatus used for the conversion of **A** to **B** in a school laboratory is drawn on the right.

   (i)   Identify the solid **Z** and state its colour.   (9)

   (ii)   Why is it important to remove the delivery tube, **W**, from the trough of water when the heating is stopped?   (6)

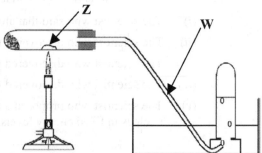

---

9. (*a*) The following words are omitted from the passage below:

Arrhenius   **neutralisation**   **hydrogen ions**   **salt**

Write in your answer book the omitted words corresponding to each of the numbers 1 to 4.   (25)

According to _____1_____ an acid is a substance that produces _____2_____ when it is dissolved in water. When an acid reacts with a base a _____3_____ reaction occurs producing a _____4_____ and water.

(*b*) The following words are omitted from the passage below:

chlorination   **flocculation**   **filtration**   **fluoridation**

Write in your answer book the omitted words corresponding to each of the numbers 5 to 8.   (25)

Aluminium salts are added to water in a waterworks to encourage suspended material to settle in a process called _____5_____. Harmful bacteria are killed in drinking water by _____6_____. In accordance with legislation _____7_____ is carried out to help prevent tooth decay. The process of passing water through sand beds is called _____8_____.

---

10. Answer any **two** of the parts (*a*), (*b*) and (*c*)   (2 × 25)

(*a*) Paper chromatography, thin-layer chromatography or column chromatography are all separation techniques.
- (*i*) Describe with the aid of a diagram an experiment to separate a mixture of indicators using any **one** of these techniques.   (18)
- (*ii*) What use is made of thin-layer chromatography in forensic science?   (7)

(*b*) The equipment drawn on the right was used in a titration between hydrochloric acid, **HCl**, and sodium hydroxide, **NaOH**.

- (*i*) Identify the pieces of equipment **A**, **B** and **C**.   (10)

- (*ii*) Which piece of equipment is used for measuring the 25 cm^3 portions of sodium hydroxide? Describe the correct procedure for washing and filling this piece of equipment.   (12)

- (*iii*) Name a suitable indicator for this titration.   (3)

A   **B**   **C**

(*c*) Magnesium burns in oxygen to produce magnesium oxide, **MgO**.

The equation for the reaction is
$$2Mg \ + \ O_2 \ \longrightarrow \ 2MgO$$

In an experiment 2.4 grams of magnesium were burned in oxygen.

- (*i*) How many moles of magnesium were burned?   (7)

- (*ii*) How many moles of oxygen were required to completely react with the 2.4 g of magnesium?   (6)

- (*iii*) What volume of oxygen does this amount of oxygen occupy at s.t.p.?   (6)
[Molar volume at s.t.p. = 22.4 litres]

- (*iv*) What mass of magnesium oxide was produced in this experiment?   (6)

---

11. Answer any **two** of the parts (*a*), (*b*) and (*c*) (2 × 25)

(*a*) The diagram on the right shows the arrangement of apparatus for a reflux.

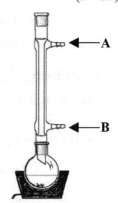

(*i*) Which of the condenser connections **A** or **B** is connected to the cold water tap? (4)

(*ii*) Why are reaction mixtures sometimes refluxed? (6)

(*iii*) Give an example of an experiment from your course where the reaction mixture was refluxed. (6)

(*iv*) Apart from the reaction mixture what else should be added to the reaction vessel before the mixture is refluxed? Why? (9)

(*b*) Define *rate of a chemical reaction.* (7)

Hydrochloric acid, **HCl**, reacts with marble, $CaCO_3$, producing carbon dioxide gas as one of the products.

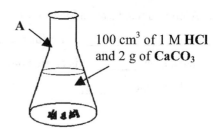

100 cm^3 of 1 M **HCl** and 2 g of $CaCO_3$

The conical flasks **A** and **B** were used in an experiment to examine the effect of concentration on the rate of a chemical reaction. Both flasks contained 2 grams of marble chips. In each case the marble chips were approximately the same size. 100 cm^3 of 1 M hydrochloric acid was added to flask **A** and 100 cm^3 of 2 M hydrochloric acid was added to flask **B**.

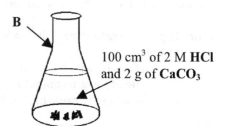

100 cm^3 of 2 M **HCl** and 2 g of $CaCO_3$

(*i*) In which flask was the reaction faster (more vigorous reaction)? Why was this reaction faster? (12)

(*ii*) Describe a test for carbon dioxide gas. (6)

(*c*) Answer part **A** *or* part **B**

A

What is the chemical formula for ozone? State **one** beneficial effect of the ozone layer. (10)

CFCs are believed to be the main cause of damage to the ozone layer.

(*i*) What are CFCs? What use is made of CFCs? (9)

(*ii*) State **one** consequence of damage to the ozone layer. (6)

or

B

Give **two** properties of transition metals. (7)

Iron can be made using the blast furnace. The diagram on the right shows a blast furnace.

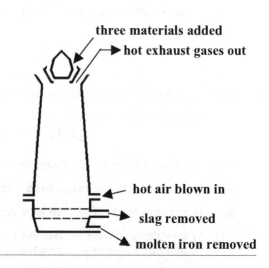

three materials added
hot exhaust gases out
hot air blown in
slag removed
molten iron removed

(*i*) Identify the **three** materials added at the top of the blast furnace. (9)

(*ii*) Write an equation for the reduction of iron oxide, Fe_2O_3, to iron in the blast furnace. (9)

AN ROINN OIDEACHAIS AGUS EOLAÍOCHTA

LEAVING CERTIFICATE EXAMINATION, 2002

CHEMISTRY - ORDINARY LEVEL

TUESDAY, 18 JUNE - AFTERNOON 2.00 to 5.00

400 MARKS

Answer **eight** questions in all

These **must** include at least **two** questions from **Section A**

All questions carry equal marks (50)

Information

Relative atomic masses: H = 1, O = 16, Cl = 35.5, Zn = 65

Molar volume at s.t.p. = 22.4 l

Avogadro constant = 6×10^{23} mol^{-1}

Section A

Answer at least <u>two</u> questions from this section [see page 1 for full instructions]

1   A sample of ethanoic acid (acetic acid) was prepared in the school laboratory as follows. A mixture of ethanol and water was added slowly from a dropping funnel into a cooled solution of sodium dichromate in concentrated sulfuric acid (Diagram 1). The mixture was allowed to warm up slowly and was then refluxed for 30 minutes.

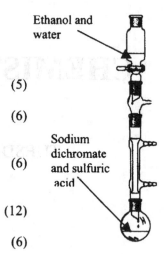

Ethanol and water

Sodium dichromate and sulfuric acid

Diagram 1

   (a)   Why was the ethanol in the dropping funnel mixed with water?   (5)

   (b)   What should be used to cool the contents of the reaction flask?   (6)

   (c)   Using a rough sketch, indicate the direction in which the water flowed through the condenser.   (6)

   (d)   What colour change occurred in the reaction mixture as the ethanol and water were added?   (12)

   (e)   Why was it important to reflux the mixture?   (6)

Following the reflux the reaction mixture was allowed to cool slightly and the apparatus was rearranged to distil the mixture (Diagram 2). A sample of ethanoic acid was isolated by distillation as the fraction which distilled off between 115 °C and 118 °C.

   (f)   What gas is given off when sodium carbonate is added to a sample of ethanoic acid? What test could you carry out to identify this gas?   (9)

   (g)   A dilute solution (5-6% w/v) of ethanoic acid (acetic acid) is used in food preservation and also as a flavouring agent. What is the common name of this solution?   (6)

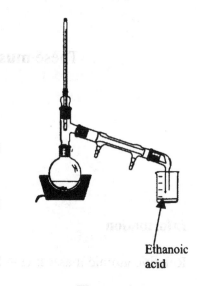

Ethanoic acid

Diagram 2

2 The concentration of a solution of hydrochloric acid was measured by titration using a standard 0.10 M solution of sodium hydroxide. The hydrochloric acid solution was titrated against 25 cm³ portions of the standard sodium hydroxide solution using a suitable indicator. The pieces of equipment shown on the right were used during the experiment.

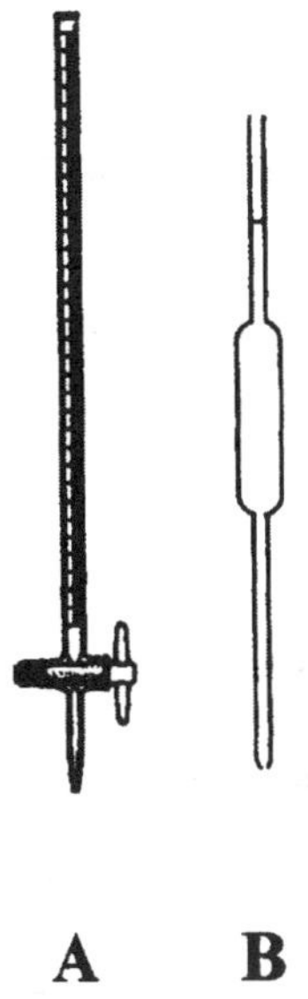

(a) Name the pieces of equipment **A** and **B**. (8)

(b) Which piece of equipment was used to measure the 25 cm³ portions of the sodium hydroxide solution?
Describe the procedure for washing this piece of equipment and for measuring the 25 cm³ portions of the sodium hydroxide solution. (12)

(c) Name a suitable indicator for this titration.
What colour change is observed at the end point? (9)

A   B

A number of accurate titrations were carried out using 25 cm³ portions of the 0.10 M sodium hydroxide solution. It was found that the mean volume of hydrochloric acid used in these titrations was 20.0 cm³. The titration reaction is described by the following equation.

$$HCl + NaOH \rightarrow H_2O + NaCl$$

(d) Calculate the concentration of the hydrochloric acid solution in moles per litre. (9)

(e) How could this experiment be extended to produce a sample of dry sodium chloride (common salt)? (12)

―――――――――――

3 Hydrogen peroxide solution decomposes rapidly into water and oxygen gas in the presence of a catalyst. When a catalyst was added to 25 cm³ of hydrogen peroxide solution, the oxygen gas produced was collected and its volume noted every 2 minutes as shown in the table.

Time/minutes	0	2	4	6	8	10	12	14	16
Volume of O_2/ cm³	0	36	54	63	68	71	73	74	74

(a) Name or give the formula of a suitable catalyst for this reaction. (5)

(b) Draw a labelled diagram of a suitable apparatus for carrying out this experiment. (12)

(c) On graph paper, plot a graph of the volume of oxygen produced (y-axis) against time (x-axis). (18)

(d) What volume of oxygen was produced during the first three minutes of the reaction?
From this calculate the average rate of oxygen production over the first three minutes of the reaction in cm³ per minute. (9)

(e) Why did the reaction slow down as time passed? (6)

―――――――――――

Section B

[See page 1 for instructions regarding the number of questions to be answered]

4   Answer **eight** of the items (a), (b), (c), etc.   (50)

   (a) Give the number of electrons in each of the main energy levels of a calcium atom.

   (b) Define *electronegativity*.

   (c) What is the shape of the ammonia molecule?

   (d) State *Boyle's law*.

   (e) Give the name <u>and</u> formula of an aromatic compound.

   (f) Balance the chemical equation

$$C_2H_4 \quad + \quad O_2 \quad \rightarrow \quad CO_2 \quad + \quad H_2O$$

   (g) The label on a bottle of mineral water indicates that 500 cm^3 of the water contains 120 mg of calcium ions. Express this concentration in parts per million (p.p.m.) of calcium ion.

   (h) Define *relative atomic mass*.

   (i) Give an example of a useful product of organic synthesis. What use is made of this product?

   (j) How many molecules are there in 9 g of water, H_2O?
      [Relative atomic masses: H = 1, O = 16; Avogadro constant = 6×10^{23} mol^{-1}]

   (k) Answer **A** *or* **B**.

     A   State **two** ways in which chemistry contributes positively to society.

     B   List **two** of the stages in the recycling of poly(phenylethene), [poly(styrene)].

---

5   Answer the questions below with reference to the following elements.

         hydrogen   **helium**   **sodium**   **oxygen**

   (a) Which of these elements is the lightest known gas?   (5)

   (b) Which element is used in yellow/orange street lights?   (6)

   (c) Which element exists as a monatomic gas?   (6)

   (d) Which of the elements has atoms with the largest atomic radius?   (6)

   (e) Which unreactive gas is mixed with oxygen for use by deep-sea divers?   (6)

   (f) Give the name <u>and</u> formula of an ionic compound formed between any two of these elements.   (9)

   (g) Draw a dot and cross diagram to show the bonding in a covalent compound formed between two of these elements. Give the name of this compound.   (12)

---

6   The compounds **A**, **B** and **C** are hydrocarbons.

$$CH_4 \qquad CH_3CH_2CH_2CH_3 \qquad (CH_3)_3CCH_2CH(CH_3)_2$$

A   **B**   **C**

(a) Which of these compounds is produced from the decomposition of animal and vegetable waste in dumps? What environmental hazard does this gas present? (8)

(b) Name each of the compounds **A**, **B** and **C**. (18)

(c) Which compound is assigned an octane rating of 100?
What problem arises in a combustion engine if the octane rating of the fuel used is too low? (12)

(d) In the past, compounds of a heavy metal were added to petrol to increase its octane rating. Name this metal. (6)

(e) Which of the three compounds **A**, **B** or **C**, is a major component of liquid petroleum gas, LPG? (6)

---

7   Mass spectrometry (MS), thin layer chromatography (TLC), gas chromatography (GC) and high performance liquid chromatography (HPLC) are all techniques used in chemistry.

(a) State **one** use that is made of mass spectrometry. (5)

(b) Describe an experiment to separate a mixture of dyes or indicators using thin layer chromatography. (18)
State **one** use that is made of this technique in forensic science. (6)

(c) Give **one** application for
    (i) gas chromatography (GC)
    (ii) high performance liquid chromatography (HPLC). (12)

(d) All of the three chromatographic separation techniques are based on the same principle. What is this principle? (9)

---

8   (a) What is *water hardness*? How can permanent hardness be removed from water? (8)

Treatment of a domestic water supply may involve each of the following stages.

sedimentation   **flocculation**   **filtration**   **chlorination**

fluoridation   **pH adjustment**

(b) In the case of any **four** of these stages, explain how the water is treated <u>and</u> state the purpose of each of these four stages. (24)

(c) Sewage treatment can be divided into three stages, **primary**, **secondary** and **tertiary** treatment. Explain what happens in each of these stages. (18)

---

9 Answer the questions below with reference to compounds **A**, **B** and **C** in the following reaction scheme.

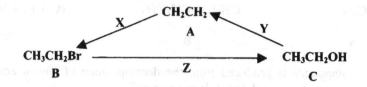

(a) Which **one** of the three compounds has only planar carbon atoms in its molecules? Draw the structure of this compound. (8)

(b) Classify the reactions **X**, **Y** and **Z** as *substitution*, *addition* or *elimination* reactions. (18)

(c) Which of the two compounds, **A** or **C**, would you expect to be more soluble in water? Give a reason for your answer. (12)

(d) Which **one** of the three compounds can be polymerised? Give **one** use of that polymer. (12)

---

10 Answer **two** of the parts (a), (b) and (c). (2 ×25)

(a) Name the female physicist, pictured on the right, who was awarded the 1903 Nobel Prize for Physics for her work on radioactivity and the 1911 Nobel Prize for Chemistry. **(4)**

She is associated with the discovery of two radioactive elements. The name of one of these elements is derived from the name of the country of her birth. Name either element. **(3)**

Alpha- (α-), beta- (β-) and gamma- (γ-) radiations are all associated with radioactivity.

(i) Place these three types of radiation in order of increasing penetrating power. (6)

(ii) Which of these three types of radiation was used by Rutherford in his experiment which led to the discovery of the nucleus of the atom? (6)

(iii) Cobalt-60, ^{60}Co, is an isotope of cobalt which emits gamma-rays (γ-rays). State **one** use made of this type of radiation. (6)

(b) Define (i) *an acid* according to the Arrhenius theory, (ii) pH. (7)

Your stomach contains a solution of hydrochloric acid which is about 0.01 M. Calculate the approximate pH of this solution. (9)

What type of compound is usually present in stomach powders used to treat acid indigestion? Name <u>or</u> give the formula of **one** such compound. (9)

(c) Ethyne (acetylene) is an *unsaturated hydrocarbon.*

What is meant by the terms (i) *hydrocarbon* and (ii) *unsaturated?* (7)

(iii) Draw a labelled diagram of the apparatus used to prepare a sample of ethyne (acetylene) gas in the school laboratory. Identify the **two** reagents used. (15)

(iv) State **one** use of ethyne gas. (3)

---

11 Answer **two** of the parts (a), (b) and (c). (2×25)

(a) State *Le Chatelier's principle*. (7)

An equilibrium mixture was set up by adding hydrochloric acid to an aqueous solution of cobalt(II) chloride. The equilibrium is described by the equation

$$CoCl_4^{2-} \ + \ 6H_2O \ \rightleftharpoons \ Co(H_2O)_6^{2+} \ + \ 4Cl^-$$

blue   **pink**

  (i) Use Le Chatelier's principle to explain the change in position of the equilibrium which results from the addition of a small amount of concentrated hydrochloric acid to the equilibrium mixture. (6)

  (ii) Given that the forward reaction is exothermic, how would an increase in temperature affect the position of the equilibrium? What colour change would accompany an increase in temperature? (12)

(b) Zinc reacts with hydrochloric acid to produce zinc chloride and hydrogen gas.
The reaction proceeds according to the following equation.

$$Zn \ + \ 2HCl \ \rightarrow \ ZnCl_2 \ + \ H_2$$

In an experiment 32.5 g of zinc were reacted with hydrochloric acid and the hydrogen gas was collected.

  (i) How many moles of zinc were used? (4)

  (ii) How many moles of hydrochloric acid were needed to react fully with this amount of zinc? (6)

  (iii) What mass of zinc chloride was produced? (6)

  (iv) What volume of hydrogen gas (measured at s.t.p.) was produced? (9)

[Relative atomic masses: Cl = 35.5, Zn = 65; molar volume at s.t.p. = 22.4 litres]

(c) Answer either part **A** *or* part **B**.

A

  (i) Name the product of the industry on which you carried out a case study.
Where in Ireland is this industry located? (7)

  (ii) Give **one** reason why this is a suitable location for the industry. (6)

  (iii) Is the production process a batch process or a continuous process? Explain your answer.
Name **one** of the raw materials used in the production process. (12)

or

B

  (i) Name the father-and-son team who received the Nobel Prize for their work in developing the X-ray technique for determining crystal structure. (4)

  (ii) Give an example of a macromolecular crystal.
Name the binding force in this crystal. State **one** use of this substance. (12)

  (iii) Give an example of a molecular crystal. Name the binding force in this crystal. (9)

AN ROINN OIDEACHAIS AGUS EOLAÍOCHTA

LEAVING CERTIFICATE EXAMINATION

CHEMISTRY - ORDINARY LEVEL

REVISED SAMPLE PAPER, FEBRUARY 2002

3 HOURS DURATION

400 MARKS

Answer **eight** questions in all

These must include at least **two** questions from **Section A**.

All questions carry equal marks (50).

Information

Relative atomic masses: H = 1, C = 12, O = 16, Na = 23.

Molar volume at s.t.p. = 22.4 l

Avogadro constant = 6×10^{23} mol^{-1}

Universal gas constant, R = 8.3 J K^{-1} mol^{-1}

1 Faraday = 96 500 C

Section A

Answer at least <u>two</u> questions from this section [see page 1 for full instructions]

1. The diagram shows the apparatus used in the preparation of
   ethyne, C_2H_2. The liquid **X** is dropped onto the solid **Y**.
   The gas is collected in test tubes as shown.

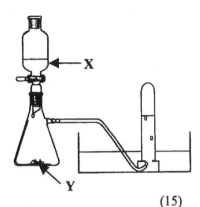

   (a) Give the name <u>or</u> formula of the liquid **X** and the solid **Y**. (8)

   (b) Describe the appearance of the solid **Y**. (3)

   (c) Why are the first few test tubes of gas collected discarded? (6)

   (d) What is observed when a sample of ethyne is burned in air? (6)

   (e) Ethyne is an *unsaturated* molecule. What does this mean?
   Describe a test you would carry out to show that ethyne is unsaturated. (15)

   (f) Draw the structure of the ethyne molecule. (6)

   (g) Give **one** major use of ethyne. (6)

   _____

2. (a) What flame colour would you observe when the following are heated in a Bunsen flame?

   (i)   A sodium salt, e.g. **NaCl** (4)

   (ii) A potassium salt, e.g. **KCl** (4)

   (iii) A lithium salt, e.g. **LiCl** (3)

   (b) Describe how you would carry out a flame test in the laboratory.
   In your answer, mention the precautions you would take to get a satisfactory result. (15)

   (c) The diagram shows the apparatus used to react a carbonate,
   e.g. **Na_2CO_3** with dilute acid, and to test the gas released.

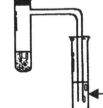

   (i) Name the gas released. (6)

   (ii) Name liquid **X** and describe the change observed
   when the gas bubbles through it. (6)

   (d) The reagents used in the "brown ring" test for nitrates are
   aqueous iron(II) sulfate and concentrated sulfuric acid.
   Describe how you would carry out this test and what you
   would observe. (12)

   _____

143

3. The apparatus shown in the diagram is used to measure the heat of reaction of hydrochloric acid, **HCl**, and sodium hydroxide, **NaOH**, solution.

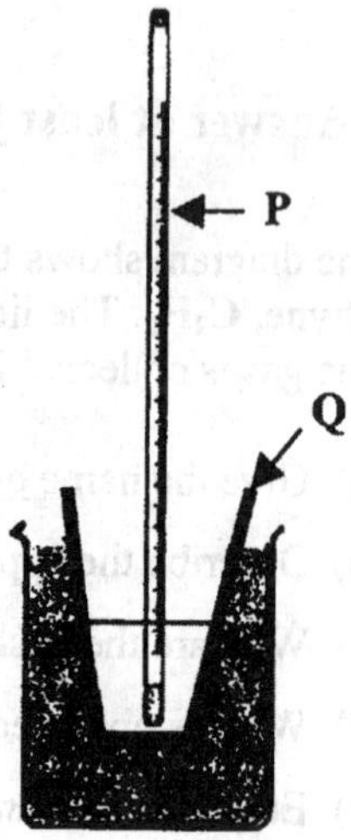

(a) Name the piece of apparatus, **P**. (5)

(b) Suggest a suitable material for **Q** and give a reason why you think this material is suitable. (12)

(c) What readings should be taken immediately before mixing the acid and base? (6)

(d) Which **two** operations are carried out using **P** after the two solutions have been placed in **Q**? (12)

(e) Sodium hydroxide is corrosive. Describe or draw the hazard symbol that should be on the label of a bottle of sodium hydroxide. (6)

When 50 cm³ of 1.0 M hydrochloric acid, **HCl** were neutralised with excess sodium hydroxide, **NaOH**, solution 2.85 kJ of heat energy were produced.

(f) Calculate the heat of reaction for the reaction between hydrochloric acid and sodium hydroxide. (9)

Section B

[See page 1 for information regarding the number of questions to be answered]

4. Answer **eight** of the following parts (a), (b), (c) etc.   (50)

(a) State *Boyle's law*.

(b) The structural formula of propene is

What is the molecular formula of propene?

(c) Ethanol is produced by *fermentation*. Explain what is meant by *fermentation*.

(d) Name an instrument that is used in the analysis of lead in water.

(e) What technique would you use to purify a sample of benzoic acid?

(f) What is the concentration, in moles per litre, of a solution that contains 4 g of sodium hydroxide, **NaOH**, per litre?

(g) Magnesium hydroxide and sodium hydrogen carbonate are both used in indigestion remedies. What chemical property makes them suitable for this purpose?

(h) Why are catalytic converters used in cars?

(i) Name the acid present in vinegar.

(j) Give **one** use of high-performance liquid chromatography (HPLC).

(k) Answer part **A** or **B**.

    A From your study of industrial chemistry, give **one** everyday example that shows why chemistry is important to society.

    B Sorting is an important step in the recycling of plastics. What simple system is used to help with this sorting?

_____

5. (a) In the modern periodic table elements are arranged in order of increasing *atomic number*.

    Define *atomic number*.   (8)

    How were elements arranged in Mendeleev's periodic table?   (6)

(b) Identify the scientists **A, B, C** and **D** in the paragraph below using names from the following list:

    Bohr   **Dalton**   **Rutherford**   **Thompson**

    A said that atoms were indivisible.
    B discovered that electrons were sub-atomic particles.
    C discovered the nucleus of the atom.
    Following this, **D** developed a model of the atom.   (12)

(c) How many (i) protons (ii) electrons are there in a calcium atom?   (6)

    State the number of electrons in each main energy level in a calcium atom.   (6)

(d) What is the general trend in atomic radii down a group in the periodic table?
    Give a reason for this trend.   (12)

_____

6. (a) The fractional distillation of crude oil in an oil refinery produced the following fractions:

gas   naphtha   kerosene   gas oil   residue

From this list, select a fraction

(i) which is used as an aircraft fuel (5)

(ii) which is the main fraction used to make petrol. (6)

Lead compounds were used to increase the *octane number* of petrol.

(iii) What is meant by the *octane number* of a fuel? (6)

(iv) Why has the use of lead in petrol been discontinued? Give another method, other than the addition of lead compounds, of increasing the octane number of petrol. (12)

(b) Butane, C_4H_{10}, is used in camping gas cylinders. Butane burns in oxygen to give carbon dioxide and water according to the equation

$$C_4H_{10} + 6\tfrac{1}{2}O_2 \rightarrow 4CO_2 + 5H_2O$$

In cooking a meal 29 g of butane gas was burned.

(i) How many moles of butane were burned? (9)

(ii) How many moles of carbon dioxide were produced? (6)

(iii) What volume does this amount of carbon dioxide occupy at s.t.p.? (6)

[Relative atomic masses: H = 1, C = 12; Molar volume at s.t.p. = 22.4 litres]

---

7. Examine the reaction scheme and answer the questions which follow:

$$CH_3CH_2OH \xrightarrow{\ \ X\ \ } CH_2CH_2 \xrightarrow{\ \ Y\ \ } CH_3CH_2Cl$$

$$A \qquad\qquad\qquad B \qquad\qquad\qquad C$$

(a) Which **one** of these compounds has planar carbons? Draw the structure of this molecule. (8)

(b) Name the compounds **A**, **B** and **C**. (12)

(c) Classify the reactions **X** and **Y** as either *addition*, *elimination* or *substitution* reactions. (9)

(d) Draw a fully labelled diagram of the apparatus used in a school laboratory to carry out the conversion labeled **X**. (15)

(e) What reagent is used to carry out the conversion labelled **Y**? (6)

---

8. A crystal of sodium chloride, **NaCl**, contains sodium ions, Na^+, and chloride ions Cl^-.

(a) What type of bond holds these ions together in a crystal? (5)

(b) State **one** property of sodium chloride which is due to the strength of these bonds. (6)

(c) Give **two** everyday uses of sodium chloride. (6)

The type of bonding in a molecule of fluorine, F_2, is different from that in sodium chloride.

(d) Name the type of bonding in fluorine. Would you expect fluorine to be more soluble or less soluble in water than in cyclohexane? (12)

(e) Would you expect sodium chloride to be more soluble or less soluble in water than in cyclohexane? Give a reason for your answer. (9)

(f) Describe a simple experiment to show that water is a polar liquid. (12)

146

9. (a) (i)   What is added to a water supply to help prevent tooth decay?   (5)

       (ii) Why is chlorine added to drinking water?   (6)

       (iii) If the pH of a reservoir water sample was 5.2, name a substance that might be added to increase the pH
             to around 7.   (6)

       (iv) One litre of water from a well was analysed by a student. The student filtered the litre of water using a
            weighed filter paper. After filtering and drying to a constant mass, the mass of the filter paper had
            increased by 0.22 g. Calculate the total suspended solids in p.p.m. (mg l^{-1}).   (9)

    (b) Sewage treatment can be carried out in three stages, **primary, secondary** and **tertiary** treatment.

       Which stage involves

       (i)   the biological breakdown of the material present in the sewage,   (6)

       (ii) mainly screening and settling   (6)

       (iii) the removal of nutrients such as nitrates and phosphates?   (6)

       What problem is associated with the release of nitrates and phosphates into rivers and lakes?   (6)

---

10. Answer **two** of the following (a), (b) and (c). (2×25)

    (a) (i)   Calculate the number of grams in 0.1 moles of anhydrous sodium carbonate, **Na$_2$CO$_3$**.   (4)

       (ii) Using the mass calculated above, describe how you would make 1 litre of a 0.1 M solution of sodium
             carbonate.   (12)

    In a titration 25.0 cm^3 of the 0.1 M sodium carbonate solution was neutralised using 20.0 cm^3 of
    hydrochloric acid solution. The equation for the reaction is

    $$\text{Na}_2\text{CO}_3 + 2\text{HCl} \rightarrow 2\text{NaCl} + \text{H}_2\text{O} + \text{CO}_2$$

       (iii) Find the molarity of the hydrochloric acid solution.   (9)

    (b) In the Haber process, nitrogen and hydrogen react to form ammonia, **NH$_3$**

    $$\text{N}_{2(g)} + 3\text{H}_{2(g)} \rightleftharpoons 2\text{NH}_{3(g)}$$

    Le Chatelier's principle is applied in deciding the best conditions for manufacture.

       (i)   State *Le Chatelier's principle*.   (7)

       (ii) What does the symbol $\rightleftharpoons$ represent?   (6)

       (iii) Write the equilibrium constant expression for the above system.   (6)

       (iv) What would be the effect of increasing the pressure on an equilibrium mixture of nitrogen, hydrogen
            and ammonia?   (6)

    (c) Hydrogen peroxide solution decomposes rapidly into water and oxygen gas in the presence of a catalyst.
        When a catalyst was added to 100 cm^3 of a solution of hydrogen peroxide, the oxygen gas produced was
        collected and its volume (V) noted every 20 seconds as shown in the table.

Time/s	0	20	40	60	80	100	120
V/cm^3	0	42	63	74	79	82	82

       (i)   On graph paper, plot the volumes of oxygen liberated (y-axis) against time (x-axis).   (15)

       (ii) From the graph find the volume of oxygen liberated after 35 seconds.   (6)

       (iii) How long does it take for the reaction to be completed?   (4)

11. Answer **two** of the following (a), (b) and (c). (2×25)

(a) (i) What is meant by chromatography?   (7)

   (ii) Describe an experiment you would carry out to separate a mixture of dyes.   (12)

   (iii) What type of chromatography is used in the analysis of samples in the drug testing of athletes and in
        blood alcohol testing?   (6)

(b) Radioactive sources can emit α-, β-, and γ-radiation.
    Arrange these types of radiation in order of <u>increasing</u> penetrating power.   (7)

   Who discovered

   (i) the elements polonium and radium   (6)

   (ii) that a photographic plate wrapped in black paper became fogged when left near a uranium salt?   (6)

   (iii) which of the radioisotopes ^{241}Am, ^{14}C, ^{60}Co, is an α-emitter?
        Give a household use of an α-emitter.   (6)

(c) Answer part **A** *or* part **B**

   A Explain the difference between *batch* and *continuous* processes in the chemical industry.   (7)

      In relation to the case study you have completed answer the following questions.

      (i) Identify the raw material(s) used.

      (ii) Name the product produced.

      (iii) Write an equation for **one** of the reactions involved.

      (iv) Give **one** use of the product.   (18)

or

   B State **one** use of low-density poly(ethene).   (4)

      Give a brief account of how low-density poly(ethene) was discovered.   (12)

      Name **one** other petroleum-based polymer and state **one** major use of that polymer.   (9)

_____

_____

Alternative Question 4 part (n) for use in Year 2

(n)   Answer part **A** <u>or</u> **B**

A Explain briefly how a greenhouse gas can cause global warming.

B What is the principal raw material used in the electric arc process for steel manufacture?

Alternative Question 11 (c) for use in Year 2

A   Nitrogen and oxygen are the major component gases in air.

(i) Explain how oxygen can be separated from air.   (7)

Atmospheric nitrogen has to undergo *fixation* before it can be used by plants.
(ii) What is *nitrogen fixation*? Give an example of how nitrogen fixation occurs in nature.   (9)

Ozone is present in the outer atmosphere.
(iii) What is ozone? Why is it important?   (9)

B   What is the *electrochemical series*?   (7)

Describe an experiment to compare the reactions of sodium and calcium with water.
State what you would expect to observe in each case and the conclusion you would make from your observations.
State <u>one</u> precaution you would take when carrying out this experiment.   (18)

Information

Relative atomic masses: H = 1, C = 12, O = 16.

Molar volume at s.t.p. = 22.4L

Avogadro constant = 6×10^{23} mol^{-1}

Universal gas constant, R = 8.3 J K^{-1} mol^{-1}

1 Faraday = 96 500 C

LEAVING CERTIFICATE EXAMINATION

CHEMISTRY – ORDINARY LEVEL

Additional Questions – May 2001

The following are examples of the type of questions appropriate to Section A on the examination paper.

Sample Question

An experiment was carried out to find the concentration of a sodium hydroxide solution. The sodium hydroxide was measured in 25.0 cm^3 portions and titrated with a standard solution of hydrochloric acid.

(a) What piece of equipment is used to transfer the sodium hydroxide solution?
Describe how it is washed before use. (11)

(b) What piece of equipment is used to measure the hydrochloric acid solution during the titration?
Apart from the washing procedures, mention <u>one</u> precaution that should be taken to ensure an accurate measurement. (9)

(c) Name a suitable indicator for this titration. What colour change would be seen at the end-point of the titration? (9)

The titration reaction is:

$$HCl + NaOH \rightarrow NaCl + H_2O$$

(d) After two accurate titrations, the mean titre was calculated to be 22.5 cm^3 of the hydrochloric acid solution. The **HCl** concentration was 0.1 M. Calculate the concentration of the sodium hydroxide solution in terms of molarity. (9)

(e) A further titration was carried out using the same solutions to prepare a sample of common salt, sodium chloride.
(i) State <u>one</u> clear difference in procedure from the previous titrations. (6)
(ii) How could a dry sample of salt be produced after this last titration? (6)

Sample Question

Anhydrous sodium carbonate can be used as a *primary standard*.

(i) What is meant by a primary standard. (6)

(ii) What mass of anhydrous sodium carbonate is needed to make up one litre of a 0.05 M solution of **Na$_2$CO$_3$**. (6)

(iii) Describe how you would make up this solution accurately. (12)

(iv) Describe how you would measure accurately 25.0 cm^3 portions of the sodium carbonate solution for use in a titration. (11)

In a titration 0.05 M sodium carbonate solution was measured out in 25.0 cm^3 portions and titrated with a hydrochloric acid solution. The mean volume of hydrochloric acid used was 22.7 cm^3.

The titration reaction is:

$$Na_2CO_3 + 2HCl \rightarrow 2NaCl + H_2O + CO_2$$

(v) Calculate the concentration of the hydrochloric acid solution in terms of molarity. (6)

(vi) Name a suitable indicator for the titration.
What colour change would be seen at the end-point of the titration? (9)

The following are examples of the type of question appropriate to Section B on the examination paper.

Sample Question

Hydrochloric acid (HCl) reacts with marble (CaCO₃), releasing carbon dioxide (CO₂) as one of the products. The reaction is represented by the equation:

$$CaCO_3 + 2HCl \rightarrow CaCl_2 + H_2O + CO_2$$

Three conical flasks, **A, B,** and **C,** were used in an experiment to examine the factors which influence the rate of a chemical reaction. In the first experiment 100 cm³ of 2 M hydrochloric acid solution was added to each of the flasks followed by a 10 g sample of marble, as described in the diagram. A stop watch was used to measure the time taken for the release of carbon dioxide to cease.

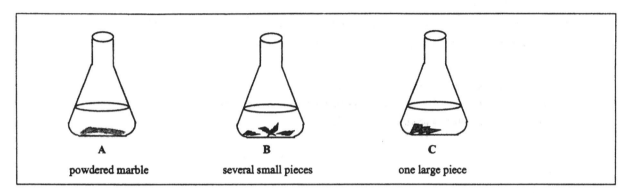

A	**B**	**C**
powdered marble	several small pieces	one large piece

(i) Which one of the three reacted fastest? Why?

    What evidence was seen to support this choice?   (18)

(ii) Which reaction was the last to finish?   (3)

In a similar set of experiments to examine the effect of concentration on rate of reaction, 100 cm³ portions of 0.5 M, 1 M and 2 M hydrochloric acid were placed in the three conical flasks and 10 g of marble chips of similar size added to each.

(iii) Why is it important to use similar sized marble chips in each case?   (6)

(iv) Which one of the experiments would you expect to finish in the shortest time?

    Give a reason for your answer.   (9)

(v) Describe how you would carry out a similar set of experiments to examine the effect of temperature on reaction rate.   (14)

Sample Question

(a) According to the Arrhenius theory, what is an acid? (8)

Sulfuric acid, H_2SO_4, is a common laboratory acid.

Give two of its chemical properties. (6)

Give an example of a household acid. (3)

(b) The pH scale is used to measure the acidity of a solution. One method of measuring pH uses an electrochemical cell, with a reference electrode and a working electrode.

(i)   What is this instrument called? (6)

(ii) Using this instrument, or otherwise, explain how you would test a solution to find its pH. (9)

(iii) Calculate the pH of a 0.1 M solution of sodium hydroxide, **NaOH**. (6)

(c) Neutralisation occurs when an acid reacts with a base.

Apart from water, what type of compound is formed in a neutralisation reaction? (6)

Give an everyday example of a neutralisation reaction. (6)

Sample Question

Methane gas, a member of the alkanes, is an important fuel. There are many sources of methane.
It can, for example, be produced in refuse dumps by the decomposition of organic waste.

(i)   Name a modern instrument which can be used to analyse gases from a refuse dump. (4)

(ii)   Apart from refuse dumps, name another significant source of methane. (6)

(iii) To which environmental problem does the escape of methane contribute? (6)

(iv)   Would you expect methane to dissolve better in water or in cyclohexane? Give a reason for your answer. (9)

(v)   What shape is a molecule of methane? (4)

(vi)   Like methane, 2-methylpropane is also an alkane. Draw its structural formula. (6)

(vii) Name an aromatic compound **and** draw its structural formula. (9)

(viii) Name a common aromatic medicine, which is used as a pain killer. (6)
